# FALLING INTO GOODNESS
## LENTEN REFLECTIONS

CHUCK DEGROAT

*Christ's love sees us with terrible clarity and sees us whole. Christ's love so wishes our joy that it is ruthless against everything in us that diminishes our joy.*

Frederick Buechner, *Wishful Thinking*

# CONTENTS

# ACKNOWLEDGMENTS

Lent comes from the Old English word *Lencten,* which means Springtime. In this season, one begins to see the goodness which emerges from the darkness of Winter. But the darkness of Winter is necessary for the greening of Spring. In this, my fourth book, I am grateful for the women and men who've walked with me through Winter seasons into the hope of Spring. You know who you are. You are not only believers in the death and resurrection of Jesus, but witnesses to that transformative journey in the lives of others, including me. You chose not to bail me out, but to let me fall, recognizing that the ground is where I'd discover my glorious limits, my creatureliness, my oneness and worthiness in Jesus. You invited me to *FALL INTO GOODNESS.*

# RETURN TO THE GROUND

## Ash Wednesday

*All go to one place; all are from the dust, and all turn to dust again. Ecclesiastes 3:20*

Ash Wednesday may be the most formative day of my year. On Ash Wednesday, we hit RESET. On Ash Wednesday, we return to the ground.

I don't like the ground. I've designed my reality so that I can avoid the ground. I hover three feet above the ground at all times, resolved to avoid the calamities, the humiliations, the shame of life on the ground. The pace of my life, the avoidance of my pain, my perfectionistic tendencies – *all* reveal my fear of the ground.

When I was young, I remember Ash Wednesday as a rather morbid affair. I recall it as a day when pastors hammered the message of human sinfulness into our stubborn ears. I imagined the pastor waking up that morning like a delighted little child, anxious for this Lenten season of sanctioned guilt-driven preaching. To my young mind, the whole dark season felt like a manipulative ploy led by robed and hooded "sour-faced saints"[1] scheming to remind Christians just how scandalously sinful they really are. I didn't know why we couldn't just skip to Easter.

No one ever told me.

No one ever told me about the power of these words:

*You are dust, and to dust you shall return.*

No one ever told me what a gift it would be to return to the ground of my being, to relinquish the exhausting attempt to fly just a bit above everyone else, to relax my fatigued ego. No one ever told me that Lent was an invitation to rest.

Have you heard about this gift to us, to the church, called Ash Wednesday? Could it be a gift to you, as well?

For years as a pastor, I had the extraordinary privilege of imposing ashes on foreheads. Sometimes I longed to say, "It's alright…come on down. Return to your ground. It's so much easier down here."

On the ground and in the dust there is no façade. No more hiding. Only rest.

And it's where Jesus can find you. Jesus came down, you see. To the dust. In the flesh. And so, you no longer need to prove yourself or protect yourself. There is no ladder to climb, no stairway to the pearly gates, no performance strategy, no purity ritual.

Only surrender. Only rest.

"Come to me, all you who are weary," Jesus says. "Not up there…down here!"

No more ladders. No more climbing. Into the dust, where God meets you and renews you.

———————

Prayer:

*Creator God, you made me from the dust, but that has not always been a pleasant thought. Can you help me imagine dust as a welcome place, however, where I'm enough, just as I am, just as you've created me, just as you hold me in Jesus? I long for the rest this might bring. Amen*

## Thursday after Ash Wednesday

*You will not die; for God knows that when you eat of it your eyes will be opened, and you will be like God, knowing good and evil. Genesis 3:4-5*

My limitations frustrate me.

From an early age I didn't quite like myself. I was too skinny. My ears were big. At bedtime, I tried to tape them back, in fact, hoping they'd find their way into a more normal position. (It didn't work.)

Sometime around middle school we wake up like Adam and Eve in the Garden to our limitations. We begin comparing. We take notice of our awkward bodies. We feel the sting of shame. And perhaps we even hear the whisper of the serpent, our budding false self, saying, "We can re-brand. Different clothes. A new attitude. Cooler friends."

We learn at an early age to despise the beauty of our dusty humanity, our creatureliness, our limitations.

By college, we're editing résumés in ways that highlight our strengths and hide our failures. We include "graduated *cum laude*" but surely don't include "got through it on Xanax, beer, and a few too many one-night stands." The self we present to the world is polished for display. Our insecure, fearful, ashamed selves are boxed and stored away, often until mid-life (unless a therapist gets a hold of us first!)

And yet, here is the invitation of Lent. If you can wake up in time to the myth of your polished and poised self, you might just realize that the fullness of your God-created, God-imaged self is waiting for you, waiting to reveal beauty, waiting to shed tears, eager for a long-awaited homecoming. You might reconnect with parts of yourself that hunger for the nourishment of Christ-within, loving and caring for each.

You, the big eared kid, are loved. You, the bucked-tooth one, are loved. You, the plain-Jane, are loved. You, the abuse victim, are loved. You, the scared little girl, are loved. You, the last-picked for the team, are loved. You, the deeply insecure star quarterback, are loved. You, who cut your wrists, are loved.

And, you might even discover that as you embrace your limitations, Jesus is already there, waiting to embrace every weary, broken, and unloved part of you. You might discover that in trying to be like God, you actually distanced yourself from God. But in embracing your humanity, you are connected to the fully human One who sets you free from the burden of being someone you are not.

---

Prayer:

*Loving God, how can it be that my limitations do not disappoint you? I have lived too long believing that I am not enough, but I ask you to enliven my imagination into the extraordinary truth that you embrace every part of me in Jesus. Will you meet me in every limitation I experience? Amen*

### Friday after Ash Wednesday

*Then the LORD God formed man from the dust of the ground and breathed into his nostrils the breath of life; and the man became a living being. Genesis 2:7*

Theologians for millennia have been fond of the language of "original sin" to describe humanity's broken condition. Fair enough. The great country parson and poet, George Herbert, once wrote, "I cried when I was born and every day shows why."[2] There is an unmistakable brokenness in the world. We see it every day in systems embroiled in racism, politics of self-interest, war, poverty, rampant consumerism, and more.

More and more, however, I find myself speaking of original creatureliness. From the dust we came. From the ground we arose. And into this dusty earth God breathed his life-giving Spirit, animating us and lifting us and ennobling us into ambassadorship as his image-bearers. But our origins are humble, nevertheless. We are *humus,* of the earth, the humble ones.

This original creatureliness is your birthright and greatest gift. It is not a picture of your badness, though. You see, some of us are quite obsessed with feeling bad about ourselves. We may even adopt a theology that emphasizes just how awful we are. One minister even told me, "we need to be reminded of our sinful lowliness every day." The poor man was one of the crankiest Jesus-followers I've ever met.

I don't know if you recall this, but when God looked upon everything he made he said it was all "very good." Not mediocre. Not "I could have made their ears look a bit less awkward." Not "I should have gone with three nostrils." No…very good! No qualifications. No revisions. He adored what he made.

Our human problem – called "sin" – is that we run from our original creatureliness, we flee our "very good" design. And when we run from it (by trying to become something we're not) we disrupt and even mock the divine design, with ripple effects throughout the whole world. From Cain's murder of Abel to racist systems today, sin's original bite reverberates.

So, here is today's invitation to you: embrace your creatureliness. Admit your limitations. Acknowledge the ways in which you've tried to avoid them. And hear the Spirit whisper to you:

*You are enough, just as God created you, just as you are.*

---

Prayer:

*Loving God, how can it be that my limitations do not disappoint you? I have lived too long believing that I am not enough and seeking my enoughness elsewhere. But I ask you to enliven my imagination into the extraordinary truth that you embrace every part of me in Jesus. Will you meet me in every limitation I experience? Amen*

## Saturday after Ash Wednesday

*Son, you are always with me, and all that is mine is yours. Luke 15:31*

"Well, it's the first Saturday of Lent…I guess I can't have too much fun today," said a long-time churchgoer in the first church that I served as a pastor. He told me that he had given up chocolate and alcohol for Lent, and asked me what I had given up this year.

"I've given up being inattentive," I said. He looked at me confused, as if this was some sort of ploy to get out of doing the real work of Lenten self-discipline.

The reality is, my heart is so fickle and so easily satisfied by cheap imitations of Love that I'd have to give up just about everything good-and-God-given to do Lent 'right.' But maybe Lent isn't about giving up our favorite treats or doing self-discipline right.

Perhaps Lent is about becoming aware – through daily attentiveness - to the reality that we are created-from-the-dust-living-spirits, that we are enough, that everything we need and long for is already ours in Christ.

When the young rebellious son returned to his father after squandering his inheritance (Luke 15), his father didn't put him through a behavior modification program. In a revolutionary act of love, the father gave him a ring, a robe, new sandals, and a welcome home feast. *Enjoy!*

I wonder how long it took the son to believe this.

I wonder how many times after that he sabotaged his father's love – "Dad, what can I do to prove it to you?"

I wonder about the mental and behavioral gymnastics we go through to prove our love, too.

His father gave him back the very ordinary, creaturely things to remind him, once again, not only that he was human, but that he was his son. In simple gestures – a ring, a robe, sandals, and a feast – he was communicating to him that he'd not fallen out of favor but he'd fallen into goodness.

In the meantime, his older brother burned with anger. He was living a perpetual toxic form of Lent, striving to be the ever-dutiful son, proving to his father that he loved him by giving up the pleasures of the world. He could not fathom his father's generosity and delight. For him, faith was a meritocracy, and he was winning. And yet, his father comes to him and says, "Everything I have is yours." Just look around. Touch it. Taste it. Experience it. This isn't a ladder-climbing exercise in self-discipline, but an awakening to the reality that you, in all your brokenness, are unfathomably loved. Fall into goodness, son!

Isn't it interesting that both sons questioned whether they were enough in their father's eyes? Both sons went looking elsewhere, one to parties and pleasures and another to duty and discipline. And neither found it!

It's the first Saturday in Lent. Did you wake up today thinking, "Well, it's Lent. I better make sure I don't break the rules"? Are you already wondering why you chose to give up Netflix rather than something simpler? Perhaps it's not too late to re-imagine Lent for yourself.

Everything God has is yours. Can you see it? Can you taste it? Or are you preoccupied and distracted? You need not look elsewhere. You, the one created by God, are enough. You are the beloved daughter or son.

Perhaps Lent is about paying attention. Perhaps Lent is about removing the blinders of our illusory life of self-fulfillment in order to feast on the Life that is already ours in Jesus.

---

Prayer:

*Ever present God, I am prone to wander, Lord I feel it, prone to leave the One I love. I am distracted, distant, and disconnected, plugged in to the approval of others, the stimulation of social media, the pursuit of security. Help me to rest in the abundant love that is already, infinitely mine in Jesus. Amen*

# WEEK 1

## DWELL WITH GOD

### First Sunday in Lent

*Again, the devil took him to a very high mountain and showed him all the kingdoms of the world and their splendor; and he said to him, "All these I will give you, if you will fall down and worship me." Jesus said to him, "Away with you, Satan! for it is written,*

*'Worship the Lord your God,
and serve only him.'"*

*Then the devil left him, and suddenly angels came and waited on him.*

*Matthew 4:10-11*

You can have it all. Really, you can. Someone on a commercial just told me.

The tragedy is that we believe it. We strive for it. Envy burns within as our coworker gets the promotion, our siblings gets the boat, our neighbor gets the in-ground pool. We are always looking for fulfillment on the outside, aren't we?

Jesus heard the words, too. *You can have it all!* And don't think for a moment he didn't pause. Let us not forget that Jesus was *fully* human. Jesus was not at all immune to the twinge of envy, the surge of lust, the enticement of you-can-have-it-all. Shortly before his crucifixion, he'd even agonize over his vocation: "My Father, if it is possible, let this cup pass from me" (Matthew 26:39).

Perhaps, Jesus even thought to himself, "I've heard this story before." Surging into his memory comes the recollection of a day when, gathered with other Jewish boys, he hears the original temptation story of Genesis 3 told. Images of the slithering snake, the promise of power and knowledge, and the sting of shame flood his mind. You, Jesus, can have it all.

Consider this, too. Not only is Jesus fully human, but Jesus is also fully God. He was present at creation, in creation. *In the beginning was the Word, and the Word was with God, and the Word was God.* I'm speculating here, but maybe something of his own original, Trinitarian imagination surged within the moment. Could it be that Jesus recalled the original simplicity and beauty of Eden, capturing it in words familiar to any Jew of that day:

*'Worship the Lord your God,*
*and serve only him.'"*

Maybe in that one crucial moment, Jesus remembered. Maybe in the midst of the *you can have it all* whisper, Jesus recalled – *Worship the Lord and serve only him.* Maybe he remembered his origins. Maybe he remembered his birthright. Maybe he remembered that humanity is born of the dust.

That's it, isn't it? You see, if God is God, then you don't have to be. You can give up your relentless, exhausting attempt to be more than you are – richer, sexier, stronger. You can remember that "everything I have is *already* yours." You don't need anything more. God is God, you're not, and that's that. You can remember. You can receive. You can rest, returning the humble ground of your being.

The words Jesus found in that moment were familiar ones, repeated often in his Scriptures – Deuteronomy, 1 Samuel, Isaiah, and in many other paraphrases. They are a call to remember. It was a way of saying, "Let's get back to the basics – to who I am, who you are, to who we are together." Worship is not some demand of a narcissistic God, but an invitation to be re-oriented rightly, to return to the ground of our beings, to accept the gift of the dust. Worship is the great return to our depths.

It's hard to remember. That's why we need Lent. In the midst of a world that says, "You can have it all," Jesus reminds us that we already do. We need not attain it. We need not achieve it. We, more often than not, simply fall into it.

———————

Prayer:

*Jesus, it's hard to imagine resisting that "you can have it all" voice as you did. The security you had in being God's beloved is remarkable. I long for this, too. In my head, I can believe that I have it all in you, but it's a much harder journey to live it. Will you whisper it to me regularly, by your Spirit? Amen*

## Monday Week 1

*There is no fear in love, but perfect love casts out fear; for fear has to do with punishment, and whoever fears has not reached perfection in love. 1 John 4:18*

"It feels like I just get stuck in my anxiety sometimes," he told me. "It's like I can be completely fine and relaxed, and then I get triggered. My whole body can go into a state of panic in seconds. It's like there are two of me – the relaxed me and the anxious me – and they're at war."

We all long to live in the experience of oneness and worthiness in Christ. We all long for wholeness, through and through. When we're operating from our core – our true self – it seems that nothing can overcome us.

And yet, both theologians and psychologists – and St. John in this passage! – seem to affirm a more complicated dynamic within us.[3] Truth be told, we can feel kind of fragmented at times. We can feel "not quite ourselves." It can feel like parts of us are at war.

Think about it. There are parts of you that you don't like and parts you do. There are parts that beat you up and parts that cheer you up. You might experience a conflict between parts of yourself. You might say to your spouse, "Part of me wants to go on a bike ride with you and another part of me wants to take a nap." You might even experience a more profound confusion, even a sense of hypocrisy, as theologian and pastor Dietrich Bonhoeffer expresses:

Who am I? This or the other?
Am I one person to-day and to-morrow another?
Am I both at once? A hypocrite before others,
And before myself a contemptibly woebegone weakling?[4]

In this passage, love and fear compete for a place of primacy within. Of course, we long to live in perfect "wholehearted" love. But fear often wins out. Fear about the conversation that went bad this morning. Fear about the big date. Fear about what you'll get back on tax day. Fear about the test results.

But perfect love casts out all fear, right? I just need to be more perfect, right? Wrong.

What St. John is getting at is not some kind of moral perfection, but a sense of oneness, of unity within, of wholeheartedness. It's as if he's aware of what psychologists know today – that we can become disconnected from our core self. He's revealing to us that we can become fragmented, disconnected from our true selves dwelling in love, dwelling in Christ. Just like the man I mentioned above, we can get triggered, becoming one with our fear and alienated from Jesus.

Now hear this: St. John isn't trying to shame you in this passage. He's not asking you to "get over" your fear. In fact, I think he's actually on to the ancient wisdom - that we're more than our anxiety. I think he's actually tuned into the reality that we were created in Love and for Love. I think he's asking us to return to our roots, to fall back into the goodness of God's original love, to a place of original fearlessness.

St. John believes that your deepest being is made for love and lives in love because he knew, very personally, Love incarnate – Jesus. But remember - he also knew fear. He watched as Jesus was hung from the Cross. So, he's not looking to shame you, but to invite you – back into Love's arms, back into Love's security, back into Love's goodness.

In the end, fear is a product of control. Parts of us vying for control within send our system into a panic, and we're quickly disconnected from our true self in Christ and thrown into a state of inner emergency. But surrender is the antithesis of control.

So, surrender to love. Fall into goodness. His arms are wide open, waiting to catch you.

———————

Prayer:

*Loving God, I admit it – I get scared. Fear seems to take over my being at times. I'm beginning to realize that I can't conquer or control fear, but I can surrender. I can fall back into the Love that is more original than fear. Teach me to fall, Jesus. Amen*

## Tuesday Week 1

*But you are not in the flesh; you are in the Spirit, since the Spirit of God dwells in you. Romans 8:9*

"How do I know that I'm living out of my true self in Christ?" she asked, frustrated by her lack of consistency in her spiritual journey. It's a good question, and it's the *right* question. Too often, our questions revolve around whether or not we're doing the 'godly' thing, living behaviorally in a faithful and obedient way. But my friend was asking a more profound question – How do I know that I'm living out of my deepest identity, my "true self" in Christ?

For St. Paul, it seems that the true self is the *Christ*-self, God hidden and dwelling within us by the Spirit. You may know it when you experience it – moments of compassion and connection to God and others, inclinations to self-giving love, a heart quickened to extend grace, to forgive effortlessly. You may also be thinking, "Why is this such an infrequent experience for me?" Don't worry, I feel the same way! I can feel so conflicted within.

I've actually learned to develop some inner dialogue around these competing parts. When I'm feeling especially judgmental of someone, I'll sometimes pause and imagine a conversation within between my true self and this angry part of me. I'll imagine Jesus, joined in union with my deepest self, showing compassion, listening well, showing curiosity. A recent dialogue went something like this:

*Me (In Jesus!): You seem very angry. What's going on?*

*Angry Part: I was misunderstood…again. I'm so mad.*

*Me: Tell me some more about it.*

*Angry Part: This friend made a huge assumption about my motives and his words felt condescending and judgmental. I'd love to fire an email away at him and tell him what I think and how wrong he is.*

*Me: Thanks for saying that. I'm so sorry that happened. Take a few minutes to relax and breathe, and know that I'm here with you. I love you.*

*Angry Part: I've taken some time now to breathe. I feel less angry knowing you see me and understand.*

Now, the first time I tried this I felt somewhat silly, and wondered if I was schizophrenic. Let me assure you, however...I'm not and you're not. We do experience inner conflict, however. There are parts of us that can feel angry, ashamed, misunderstood, frightened, abandoned. There are parts of us that may feel very young and vulnerable. These parts of us need the care of Christ in unique ways. In fact, with some practice you might find yourself engaging in meaningful and healing inner conversations around these different parts of you.

So, what is the true self like? A favorite psychologist of mine uses 7 c's to describe the true self: calm, compassionate, courageous, clear, creative, curious, connected.[5] I find it interesting that psychologists are discovering attributes of this true self that are beautifully analogous to the fruits of the Spirit! What if psychology has accidentally discovered that life in the Spirit is actually the most healthy, vibrant, soul-nourishing life there is?

You are in the Spirit. Christ dwells in you. It may not always feel like it. You might be triggered to anger, flooded with shame. But it's your deepest reality. Beneath your brokenness is a profound goodness – God dwelling within.

---

Prayer:

*Compassionate Spirit, you are more kind to me than I imagined. It is astounding to imagine that you dwell in me, longing to heal my many inner conflicts. I've got work to do, but knowing that you are listening and loving within is such an encouragement. Thank you for your kindness to me. Amen*

## Wednesday Week 1

*Do you not know that your body is a temple of the Holy Spirit within you, which you have from God, and that you are not your own? 1 Corinthians 6:19*

When I heard this verse quoted in my childhood, the application dripped with guilt. In my imagination, old St. Paul was a prude man shouting in my face warnings of sexual sin. I only have anecdotal evidence for it, but I'd contend that this text is quoted most in books on sexual addiction and sermons on adultery.

But if we move too quickly to behavioral maxims, we miss the beautiful imagery and theological rationale behind caring for our bodies. Our bodies are *temples*. No, not sinful and fleshy repositories of a soul. No, not dirty prisons. *Temples*.

Temples, of course, are the domain of gods. The tabernacle/temple elaborated in the Old Testament was, in various accounts, the center of the earth, God's new Eden, the dwelling place of the King, and the staging ground out of which the entire earth would be renewed and restored.

Monks and hermits who went out into the desert in the early centuries of the church took this imagery seriously. Their desert vocation was to do the challenging heart work of knowing oneself, of examining motives, and of preparing the heart as the King's palace. A 4th century monk – St. Macarius – paints a beautiful picture, writing:

Within the heart is an unfathomable depth. There are reception rooms and bedchambers in it, doors and porches, and many offices and passages. In it is the workshop of righteousness and of wickedness. In it is death, in it is life. The heart is but a small vessel; and yet dragons and lions are there, and there likewise are poisonous creatures…rough, uneven paths are there, and gaping chasms. The heart is Christ's palace…there Christ the King comes to take His rest, with the angels and the spirits of the saints, and He dwells there, walking within it and placing His kingdom there…the heavenly cities and the treasures of grace: all things are there.[6]

Every time I read this passage it takes my breath away. All of that…in me?!

And yet, you and I can live such externalized lives that we miss the opportunity to enter into the depths, explore the passageways, chase the lions, and cultivate beauty. Our busy, frenetic lives find us moving from one task to the next, rarely stopping to assess our health. We remember to change the oil in our cars, change the filters in our water dispensers, and change the bag on our vacuums, but we neglect the work of inner housecleaning. We're unfamiliar with the vast territory of our hearts.

And so we tinker every now and then with a self-help book, a new behavioral strategy to lose weight or avoid porn, a Lenten fast. Soon enough, though, we're right back where we started. The cycle goes on, and eventually we feel helpless to change. Some go to therapy. Others give up the process altogether. Many bury their hearts, refusing to feel, to examine, to seek Christ in the innermost places.

If we were sitting together, I'd ask you how you've experienced this. I ask this quite a bit, in fact, and get a wide variety of responses. Some tell me that this talk of inner depths is selfish introspection. Others say that Jesus is on his throne in heaven and we should focus upward, not inward. A few talk of bad experiences with a therapist.

Others claim a lack of time. Many say, "I've never heard anything quite like this before. This could be a beautiful journey!"

Your heart is a temple. God resides there. But there are plenty of obstacles to face on your adventure inward. Dragons, lions, and poisonous creatures are apt metaphors for the many resistances within. Because my early story of faith was filled with influential adults who showed little curiosity for my heart and great interest in my behavior and theological agreement, my inner dragons will sometimes whisper, "This is nonsense Chuck. Nothing to see here. Christ wouldn't dwell in your sorry heart, anyway." I've needed friends, mentors, counselors, and spiritual directors in various stages of my journey over the last two decades of 'recovery' from these poisonous messages to encourage me, challenge me, and mostly remind me that God not only dwells within, but loves me through and through.

What might it be like for you to explore these inner realms? What are the resistances that emerge for you as you consider this temple exploration project? What are the obstacles that impede safe passage within? The journey begins with desire, an earnest desire to explore and a sincere commitment to continue despite the dragon's opposition. But the good news is this: Christ has already taken up residence, and he's calling for you, urging you on the journey, and filling you with the spiritual resources you need to make it Home.

———————

Prayer:

*Christ the King, that you sit enthroned in my heart – your temple – is a mystery to me. But it's a mystery worth exploring! I long to be Home with you, but there are many obstacles and resistances in the way. Give me the grace and the courage to journey on, and the ears to hear your voice cheering me on the way. Amen*

## Thursday Week 1

*You shall be called by a new name*
*You shall be a crown of beauty*
*and a royal diadem.*
    *from Isaiah 62*

I would not normally choose a fourth-century Trinitarian theologian as my therapist, but if Gregory of Nyssa were alive still I might ask for an appointment. Above my desk I hang a quote of his:

*Our godlike beauty is hidden behind curtains of shame.*

This is really good news for someone like me. Could it be good news for you?

The shame message is a loud one, after all. Parts of us shout, "You're not enough – thin enough, smart enough, spiritual enough, disciplined enough." Maybe this shame voice is even telling you that you don't do Lent well enough. The inner voice of shame can be relentless. It's a primary tool Evil uses to erode loving intimacy with God.

Sometimes we need long dead fourth-century theologians to come along and tell us that our deepest self is really quite beautiful to God.

*Our godlike beauty is hidden behind curtains of shame.*

Don't believe him? How about believing the greatest spiritual theologian of the 20th century, Thomas Merton? He writes:

Then it was as if I suddenly saw the secret beauty of their hearts, the depths of their hearts where neither sin nor desire nor self-knowledge can reach, the core of their reality, the person that each one is in the eyes of the Divine. If only they could all see themselves as they really are. If only we could see each other that way all the time. There would be no more war, no more hatred, no more cruelty, no more greed…I suppose the big problem would be that we would fall down and worship each other.[7]

Merton makes an even more audacious claim than St. Gregory. Not only will our shame dissipate, but war, hatred, cruelty and greed will cease. We may even begin to see each other as gods and goddesses.

In a season when our spiritual focus can become behavioral and our sense of growth tied to successful fasting from chocolate or Facebook, I'd like to suggest a different practice. What if instead of seeing your 'sinful behavior' as the big problem, you shifted your focus to your original goodness? What if instead of imagining God's disappointment in your lack of discipline you imagined God smiling at his very image in you. Yes, in you…of all people! Perhaps, that alone could stir in you a desire to live faithfully in every aspect of your life.

You see, too often we play the game of mistaken identity. You woke up one day believing that you were a lowly pauper, and many voices within your life conspired to convince you of its truth. Even some spiritual guides along the way participated in this dark conspiracy. They've become convinced that what defines us is the trinity of bentness, badness, and brokenness.

But the Trinity who created you for beauty, goodness, and dignity knows better. The Father designed you, down to that oddly placed freckle. The Son came to remind you of who you are, becoming a pauper to rescue you from indignity and despair. The Spirit was sent to be your deepest voice, your inner Counselor, whispering Beauty and Dignity over your soul day and night. Together, they long to be your homing beacon, ushering you back to your original design, reminding you of your God-imaged goodness.

Can you hear their whisper?

_____

Prayer:

*Holy Trinity, rescue me from the unholy trinity of bentness, badness, and brokenness. Release its grip on my imagination, and show me my dignity and beauty hidden beneath curtains of shame, bestowed to me by you, ever gracious One. Amen*

### Friday Week 1

*To them God chose to make known how great among the Gentiles are the riches of the glory of this mystery, which is Christ in you, the hope of glory. Colossians 1:27*

Here is the great mystery: *Christ in you.* Not a few galaxies away. Not a few continents away. Not a few miles away. Not even a few inches away. No, Christ *in* you.

Christ in you, with all of your self-sabotaging ways. Christ in you, with all of your burdening doubts. Christ in you, with all of your past infidelities. Christ in you, even in the Ash-Wednesday-dust of your creatureliness. Christ in *you*.

The story is told of the great 15th century saint, Catherine of Genoa, who was so utterly consumed by this extraordinary truth that she ran through the streets declaring, "My deepest me is you, Oh God! My deepest me is you!"[8] Can you imagine the strength and security in one who would risk humiliation to declare this profound reality?

Because we've blown it time and again, it is quite easy to believe that what resides in us is nothing but darkness. Shame in you. Pain in you. Brokenness in you. But St. Paul and St. Catherine heartily disagree. Here is the mystery: *Christ* in you.

Why does it take so long to embrace this? The hard and sad reality is that there is a conspiracy of our own self-sabotaging voices matched by the twisted obsession some pastors have with telling people how bad they are. I've often told pastoral colleagues, "You don't need to convince people that they're bad. They feel it already." We live in a shame-and-guilt saturated culture, and it doesn't take much for the old, dark internal scripts to play again. In fact, the self-esteem movement of the late-twentieth century tried to remedy this, but it only compounded our sense of unworthiness.[9]

Sin, you see, is a rejection of your original goodness. It is a sabotaging of your original beauty. It is your silly attempt to find love on the outside when the *Christ in you* reality is that it's already yours.

The great 5th century Bishop of Hippo, St. Augustine, expressed his own regret about how long it took for him to get this. As you reflect on his words, perhaps it's not too late for you not only to believe this, but to experience it in the depths of your own spirit:

*Late have I loved you, oh Beauty ever old, ever new, late have I loved you. You were within me, and I was outside myself and it was there that I sought you and, myself disfigured, I rushed upon the beautiful things you have made. You were with me but I was not with you.*[10]

―――――――

Prayer:

*Oh Beauty ever old, ever new. It has been too long. I have been busily trying to prove myself while you've been at home in me all the while. I have been frustratingly scattered in my love while you've been loving me from within all the while. Welcome me home, I pray. Amen*

## Saturday Week 1

*But in fact it is no longer I that do it, but sin that dwells within me. For I know that nothing good dwells within me, that is, in my flesh. I can will what is right, but I cannot do it. For I do not do the good I want, but the evil I do not want is what I do. Now if I do what I do not want, it is no longer I that do it, but sin that dwells within me. Romans 7:17-20*

"You're nothing – no good, good for nothing!"

It's amazing to me how many people I've pastored and counseled feel this. Executives and ex-convicts, pizza deliverers and pastors – this message does not discriminate. Success does not mitigate it. Self-helps books don't cure it. Only an encounter with the One whose yoke is easy and burden is light eases the sting of it.

There are some who will argue that this message is true, however. They're convinced that they are bad to the core, depraved sinners in the hands of an angry God. Christians who've lived in the faith for years will stake their theological integrity on it. Somehow, preserving this principle is more important than living in the truth that we are "a new creation – the old has gone, the new is here" (2 Cor. 5:17).

I grew up hearing a part of Romans 7 echoing in my ear – "nothing good dwells in you." But I've had to re-tune my hearing over time. St. Paul seems to be saying that something within me has the power to hijack my "I" – my true self. He says that it is no longer I, myself, who sins, but sin in me. Sin is a passenger who has taken control of the car, steering erratically.

But I see it. I know it. Paul seems to be saying that I (we!) want to do good, but we're stuck. On our own, it's nothing but wrong turns and dead ends.

So, to be clear – I really do want something different, according to Paul. I'm just stuck. It's not that I'm as wretched as I can be. It's not that I'm toxic to the core. No, the reality is that I – my true self – is enslaved. I'm sick with sin. But my sickness and slavery don't define me.

This is such an important corrective. As I hear Paul, what I'm struck by is that my "flesh" is my false self. It's the sin-diseased part of me that plays the contrarian, that whispers in my ear, "Surely, God didn't say that that special tree is off-limits to you!" In other words, sin is not native to my soul. It is an invader.

That's the first piece of this passage, and it's a huge one. Somehow, it's revealing a paradox. We're not as bad as we can be. We're not "bad to the bone." Sin is not our identity and does not define us. (You can wipe the sweat from your brow and smile...that's good news.)

On the other hand, we've got a problem. A disease looms large. It hijacks every form of wellness within. As the great 19th century preacher Charles Spurgeon said, sin is a "disease of the vital region," the heart. We're literally heart-sick. And some of us need to know that we're sicker than we think while others need to hear that they're not defined by their sickness. What do you need to hear?

But there's something else we need to hear before we leave St. Paul's words behind. I've discovered I can't conquer this disease on my own.

Have you tried? I have. I get into fights with parts of me that struggle for control. We throw jabs back and forth. I'll beat myself up with negative words when I don't live up to my own expectations. I'll try to overcome seemingly weaker parts of me with strict behavioral guidelines. I'll work as hard as I can until I'm pressed down under a heap of guilt and shame, unable to see my way out.

And maybe it takes this. Maybe it takes getting good and tired of trying on our own to beat back the disease of sin. Maybe it takes coming to the end of ourselves to hear what Paul says in the verses that follow:

*Who can set me free from my sinful old self? God's Law has power over my mind, but sin still has power over my sinful old self. I thank God I can be free through Jesus Christ our Lord!*

In uniting ourselves to Jesus and in surrendering control, we begin to experience freedom from the vestiges of the old, false self which takes on a hundred different personalities within us, each vying for the driver's seat. The voice of Jesus within us, present by the Spirit, becomes the powerful voice of truth, of goodness, of joy, of peace, of love. A hundred other voices may be whispering, perhaps even screaming. But, if we can tune our ears, it's just possible that we'll hear a different one than the other, toxic and negative voice, one that says, "I love you – each and every one of you – and I won't stop loving you until each and every one of you finally relaxes your grip and receives my compassion."

---

Prayer:

*Compassionate Spirit, you are more kind to me than I imagined. It is astounding to imagine that you dwell in me, longing to heal my many inner conflicts. I've got work to do, but knowing that you are listening and loving within is such an encouragement. Thank you for your kindness to me. Amen*

# WEEK 2

# LIVE FROM YOUR TRUE SELF

## Second Sunday in Lent

*But a Samaritan while traveling came near him; and when he saw him, he was moved with pity. He went to him and bandaged his wounds, having poured oil and wine on them. Then he put him on his own animal, brought him to an inn, and took care of him. Luke 10:33-34*

What does Jesus see when he sees you? What do you see in you? Take it a step further – what do you see in your neighbor?

If I understood the love of Jesus in and through my judgments of myself and others, it would not be a very generous picture. The generosity of Jesus in the Gospels stands in stark contrast to the judgments of the religious leaders. In fact, his kindness is an offense to these nit-picking moralists who go around checking theological positions and measuring behavioral conformity.

In the early centuries after Jesus, Christians took seriously the call to "follow Christ," becoming good Samaritans in ways that challenge my addiction to comfort and security. They rescued abandoned babies off of trash piles, entered plague infested towns to care for the sick as others were running away, practiced faithfulness in marriages, and pooled their resources to share abundantly. I want to believe that these early followers were not motivated by guilt ("I'm going to hell if I don't do this") but desire – desire to see the beauty and dignity of Christ fill embattled souls, renew broken cities, and enliven the spiritually dead.

In other words, they saw life amidst death, dignity amidst depravity, hope amidst despair. The pursuit of dignity motivated acts of justice, peace, and reconciliation. Now, I'm sure they were prone to judgmentalism just like you and me, but they refused to reduce people to their offenses.

A pastor and theologian named John Calvin articulated this social ethic 500 years ago when he wrote, "It is not the will of God... that we should forget the primeval dignity which (God) bestowed on our first parents – a dignity which may well stimulate us to the pursuit of goodness and justice." Calvin, who had a lot to say about human wickedness and sin, refused to define people by their sin, but urged a Jesus-like generosity to all. He admits it's difficult, but says this:

> In this way only we can attain to what is not to say difficult, but all together against nature, to love those that hate us, render good for evil, and blessing for cursing, remembering that we are not to reflect on the wickedness of men, but look to the image of God in them, an image which, covering and obliterating their faults, should by its beauty and dignity allure us to love and embrace them.[11]

What does Jesus see when he sees you? What do you see in you? What do you see in your neighbor? I can focus on the negatives, at times. In fact, it's hard for me to imagine the dignity beneath the depravity of an abusive husband, a mercilessly rude boss, a manipulative political leader, or a power-abusing pastor.

Of course, Jesus isn't encouraging an ethic that turns a blind eye toward wickedness. But it seems as if his first posture, his default gear, his initial instinct is always generosity. In the same chapter as the "Good Samaritan" story, Jesus encourages his followers to go city-to-city and show hospitality – to love and heal, to bless and bring peace. And yet, the sad reality of life in a broken world is that some will reject our generosity and sabotage the opportunity for healing. Jesus says:

> But whenever you enter a town and they do not welcome you, go out into its streets and say, 'Even the dust of your town that clings to our feet, we wipe off in protest against you. Yet know this: the kingdom of God has come near. I tell you, on that day it will be more tolerable for Sodom than for that town.

Over the years, I've tried to allow this tension to define my own ministry of pastoring, counseling, and teaching. In generosity, I pursue even those who don't seem to deserve it. I honor the image-bearing dignity in them. But some will sabotage it. In their brokenness, they will reject your hospitality and refuse your invitation for them to experience the depths of God's love.

Years ago, I walked a woman through a difficult season of marriage in which she started to take seriously the damage of her husband's alcoholism and emotional abuse. She had a remarkable capacity to see what her husband could become if he pursued health and sobriety, but despite her efforts he refused, sabotaging her generosity over and again. However, her repeated attempts to save her marriage and help her husband began to erode her own sense of dignity and worth. Eventually, with the wise counsel of friends, a pastor, and others, she decided to "wipe the dust off of her feet" and leave her toxic marriage. Some Christian friends condemned her for being unforgiving. However, we did not want to see her abusive husband continue to use and abuse her generosity, and we felt a strong need to pursue and value her dignity. She was like the man in the Good Samaritan story…robbed, beaten, half dead, and in need of care.

Living out the generosity of Jesus is a messy business. We may find ourselves going into places we never expected to visit. We may wind up forgiving people we thought unforgivable. We may also find our generosity refused and rejected. You see, we are in the Good Samaritan story, not just as givers of grace, but as broken and weary recipients of the grace of Jesus – the ultimate Good Samaritan. And so, experience his generosity. Drink deeply of it. And as you do, you'll grow in your capacity to show generosity to others and, with discernment, to walk away when your generosity is sabotaged.

———————

Prayer:

*Christ the Good Samaritan, I want to receive your generosity and I want to become one who lives with generosity. It's confusing, at times, because it is hard to believe that you see dignity and beauty behind my sin and pain. In this Lenten season of refinement, grow me up into one who wholeheartedly embraces your grace and wholeheartedly offers it to others. Amen*

## Monday Week 2

*"Do you see this woman? I entered your house; you gave me no water for my feet, but she has bathed my feet with her tears and dried them with her hair. 45 You gave me no kiss, but from the time I came in she has not stopped kissing my feet. 46 You did not anoint my head with oil, but she has anointed my feet with ointment. 47 Therefore, I tell you, her sins, which were many, have been forgiven; hence she has shown great love. But the one to whom little is forgiven, loves little.' 48 Then he said to her, "Your sins are forgiven." Luke 7:44-48*

God will love you if you love others.

It sounds true enough, doesn't it? And yet, it's a version of the same lie the serpent spewed in Genesis and Satan spewed in the wilderness to Jesus: *You can attain. You can achieve. Climb the ladder of good works to the top, and you will have proven to God that you're worth it.*

This is Evil's twisted lie. You see, love is not an achievement game, it's an act of intimacy. Love is easy – amazingly easy – when it emerges from one's deepest core. Think about one's first glimpse of a newborn. That kind of love isn't forced, isn't willed. That kind of love is a surrender to the grace and givenness of God's extraordinary gifts.

I don't know where religion twisted loving God into a performance game. I see this beautiful picture of a so-called "sinful woman" whose love is reckless and free, and wonder why we've turned loving God into a checklist of behaviors. We too often look more like the Pharisees than this prodigious lover.

Loving God is an act of intimacy, not of moral performance. It emerges from our heart's longing for connection. The most common language for this intimacy throughout the history of the church has been sexual, a fact that surprises and even embarrasses many. Think about it. The enjoyment of sexual intimacy isn't predicated on following a to-do list. It's not a burdensome duty. No, it's an encounter bathed in longing, satisfied in mutual surrender. That so many writers found Song of Solomon to be the best picture of this kind of intimacy is not shocking.

The "true self" in Christ cannot do anything but love. Its vocation is love, compassion, and connection.

Our false selves, with their fig-leaved propensity for hiding and scheming, demand love, manipulate love, sabotage love.

And Jesus sees through to the core. Jesus sees our heart's desire. Fyodor Dostoyevsky once said, "To love someone means to see them as God intended them."

Jesus seems to know how you and I sabotage and manipulate and scheme and demand, and yet...and yet...he offers grace, releasing us to live from our hidden life in Christ in fullness and joy. He sees us to the core. And he sees his image, alive with dignity and goodness.

While the religious leaders competed and compared, a woman loved. Sitting at the feet of Jesus, she bathes them, drying them with her hair! She kisses his feet. Can you imagine the scene? As the religious men tower over, she sits in the dust of Ash Wednesday, connected to the ground, not just physically but spiritually.

Can you imagine the gossip among the onlookers? And yet, Jesus recognizes prodigious love when he sees it. That's faith. Unfettered and free. Surrendered and intimate.

In a season where many typically tidy up their behaviors and tame their passions, might we instead take some time to reflect on who and what we love? Perhaps, as we give up trying so hard, we might just allow ourselves to fall into the goodness of this sacred intimacy, returning to the gracious ground in humble, prodigious love.

———————

Prayer:

*God our Prodigious Lover, you give and give and give. You seem at ease with a kind of reckless intimacy that tends to embarrass me. I prefer rules and checklists, ways of knowing that I'm actually pleasing you. Could it be that love is much more simple, intimate, and available? I'm ready to find out. Amen*

## Tuesday Week 2

*As a deer longs for flowing streams, so my soul longs for you, O God. My soul thirsts for God, for the living God. When shall I come and behold the face of God? Psalm 42:1-2*

Can you fathom living according to your sacred and holy design by God? Can you imagine honoring yourself and others in the generosity afforded to dignified image-bearers? Can you imagine feeling alive with desire, beauty-infused desire animated by your loving Creator?

We may be the only creature in this world that resists living according to its design. The tree cannot help but lift its strong limbs draped in reds and yellows and oranges into the Autumn sky. The puppy cannot help but wag its furry tail at the arrival of its master. The rock cannot help but sit still as a paperweight in obedience to its Creator.

But we put on faces that are not our own. We strive to be as fit as our coworker, as funny as our sibling, as politically-informed as our best friend. We choose someone else's design to copy, and in so doing we find ourselves disconnected from our own. I've seen this too much, both in myself and in many, many others. It is a form of impoverishment. Disconnected, we live hollow lives of imitation. What we feel, think, and do does not emerge from our truest self in God.

The Psalmist says that his soul desires God. In a world of competing desires, the Psalmist seeks to recalibrate. He holds his inner compass out and discovers his true direction, his heart's deepest longing. This is pretty astounding. The Psalmist doesn't say, "I can't trust my longings...they're always twisted and wrong." In the midst of what seems to be profound pain in the Psalm, the writer sifts through the varying emotions and tunes in. This attunement doesn't make the pain go away instantly, but it does provide a lifeline, an anchor.

In fact, it's often our lack of anchoring that gets us in trouble in the first place. The tree is content being a tree and a rock sits as a rock would sit, but we try on a thousand different masks to see which fits best. Outside the Garden, we search for our fig-leaved persona-of-the-day which we hope will allow us to shine, to outsmart, to humor, to overcome.

Sometimes, I wish I could go back to my early childhood, a time when I wasn't so worried about what others thought, a time when I lived from my own unique, quirky design unapologetically. I'm reminded of a poetic musing by Rilke:

> May what I do flow from me like a river, no forcing and no holding back, the way it is with children. Then in these swelling and ebbing currents, these deepening tides moving out, returning, I will sing you as no one ever has, streaming through widening channels into the open sea.[12]

Do you, like me, desire to be attuned to your own deepest desires, like the Psalmist? Do you desire to be like the tree that praises God, the river that flows freely, the puppy that delights at the arrival at its master? If so, speak this longing out loud. Allow the desire to well up within, especially in this Lenten season. Bring to God your longings with a sense of childlike abandon.

------

Prayer:

*Ever-present Spirit, I long to live and love with a childlike freedom. And yet, I'm constrained by the masks I've chosen to wear to cover my shame and insecurity. Awaken my fickle heart to its deepest desire — a life lived fully in you. Amen*

## Wednesday Week 2

*God blessed them, and God said to them, "Be fruitful and multiply, and fill the earth and subdue it; and have dominion over the fish of the sea and over the birds of the air and over every living thing that moves upon the earth.* Gen 1:28

Among Western Americans, Wednesday is hump-day. For those of us whose work week begins on Monday, there is the dreaded moment when the alarm sounds and the perpetual routine begins again – shower and clothes, hair and makeup, lunch and laptop, and…where are my keys? Hump-day is a half-way house of sorts, a glimpse of light on the horizon. So, how are you feeling on this hump-day?

Sadly, work is often treated as the price we pay for days off, a vacation to Florida, and the just-not-enough paycheck. Some dread it and cut corners as best they can. Others cope by trying to conquer it. Coffee sustains. Dreaming of Friday gets us over the hump. And we hit repeat.

And yet, consider this in light of Lent: your work connects you to the ground, to your ground. Whether you make latte's or trade stocks, design roadways or raise children, your work is an invitation to your creaturely humanity – your body, your hands, your sweat, your intuition, your participation in something beyond you.

Yes, I'm familiar with work's curse in Genesis 3. But I'm thinking of work's blessing in Genesis 1. I'm thinking of you – the God-imaged you – made to fill and subdue, created to exercise God's ambassadorship, to name, to bless, and to care for. I'm thinking of the opportunity to bring your whole self to a particular task, like the guy who mowed my lawn one summer once did.

He probably didn't know I was watching him, but I was. He was just another member of the crew, but he mowed like he owned the company. He steered that wide deck, stand-on mower around our yard with precision and authority, creating his signature circular patterns with delight. When he finished, he'd step away to admire his workmanship, take in the smell of freshly cut grass, and (I'm quite sure) give thanks for the job. His admiration was not rushed. He was not on to the next lawn. No, he lingered, if only to notice a spot he missed or to gather a few fallen tree branches. Somehow his work was a connection to something deep, good, and original in creation. He taught me a lot that day.

Have dominion, God says. Exercise your image-bearing wherever you are, as the royalty I've made you to be. Be my ambassador, no matter whether you preach sermons or punt footballs, flip burgers or finance startups. How great a tragedy it would be to fail to see your beauty, your creativity, your humanity shining in the ordinary stuff of life.

To be sure, this is not an invitation to settle – to settle for abusive labor or indignity, to settle for work that erodes your closest relationships and kills your soul. However, Lent may be just the season to slow down and consider what your work means. Where has God placed you? What is it teaching you? How are you exercising your ambassadorship? What beauty or dignity are you bringing into your unique space in the world? How is Christ present in the ordinariness?

In fact, Christ delights in the ordinary. Ordinary work. Ordinary you, waking up each day into gratitude for the gift of breathing Spirit-life into every space and every place you meander.

---

Prayer:

*Creator God, you designed me to be your image-bearing ambassador in whatever I do and wherever I go. I cannot imagine it! Sometimes, I wonder if what I do even matters. I pray that Christ would show up in me and through me in ordinary ways breathing Spirit-life into every space and place I meander. For the sake of your Kingdom, Amen*

## Thursday Week 2

*Your terrors have paralyzed me.*
*They swirl around me like floodwaters all day long.*
*They have engulfed me completely.*
*You have taken away my companions and loved ones.*
*Darkness is my closest friend.*

*Psalm 88:17-18*

When we live from our true selves, we live free from emotional reactivity yet ever in touch with our wide range of emotions. This is an important realization, because many believe that to be "in Christ" and to live from the new self is to live in a perpetual state of bliss.

In truth, living from the true self allows us to be radically in touch with every part of us, every emotion, even the supposed dark ones. As we cultivate a life lived from our center, however, we become free from the stranglehold of particular emotions or emotional states. Our addictive habits, patterns and emotions release their grip, allowing us to live non-reactively and freely from a place of honesty and vulnerability.

Someone I saw for counseling experienced the vice grip of seething anger after a divorce. For several years, her anger occupied a center seat in her psyche, conducting her internal orchestra for her. She later said to me that it felt as if she was possessed by it. The anger overflowed into her parenting, her work, even her most intimate relationships.

When she came to me she said that a previous therapist told her that the anger needed to be expressed. This was true, but years of repressed rage came flooding in to such an extent that in time she fired her therapist in a fit of rage.

When the Psalmists express emotions of anger, sadness, loneliness, abandonment, fear and more, what they are demonstrating for us is how emotions brought into the light of vulnerable relationship with God can be released into God's secure hands rather than held tightly. They are teaching us surrender, possible only because we're living from our God-self, united to Jesus, where compassion for every emotion is possible.

My client's anger took over because she was not quite ready to plunge into the depths of her rage. Her life had been a whirlwind of dominating emotional states – fear, depression, addiction. Opening the floodgates of rage simply gave another part of her free access to take over.

Cultivating a deep, experienced union with Christ anchors us for the hard work of honoring our many fluctuating emotions. When we embrace the stunning reality that the Spirit dwells within, something within us is opened. We're not alone. We're held, secure, anchored. We experience peace amidst the storms of life.

God's Spirit is no stranger when "darkness is our closest friend." God is no stranger to every emotion within. When our true self united with Christ listens within, it can hear the painful voices calling out from within, the many emotions that need to be expressed. And as a result, we can choose to give parts of us a voice, even a Psalm, if that seems best.

Allow Lent to be a season where you cultivate a deep, anchored centeredness in which your new-creation-self in Christ can tune in compassionately to every emotion within and give them a voice.

---

Prayer:

*Spirit of God, can I trust that you dwell in me so deeply that no emotion, no thought, no behavior is a surprise to you? Could it be possible that I could find that center to be such an anchoring place that I can join your Spirit in extending compassion to myself? May it be so. Amen*

## Friday Week 2

*The fruit of the Spirit is love, joy, peace, patience, kindness, generosity, faithfulness, gentleness, and self-control. Galatian 5:22-23*

"Exercise a bit more self-control," I heard her yell to her 5 year old in the frozen foods section of the grocery store. He was walking down the aisle opening each door and slamming it shut. One by one he continued until he stepped right in front of me and slammed the door I had already opened.

The adorable little punk actually got me thinking about what self-control really is that day. Like a bolt of lightning, it hit me – Self-control is when our true selves, in Christ, are in control. Self-control isn't a strict behavior-modification project – it's simply living from our center.

Lent is often a season where the term self-control is thrown around. Having indulged on Fat Tuesday, we enter Ash Wednesday with a sense that this is the season to get right again – lose the weight, end the pornography addiction, clamp down on drinking. Someone once said to me, "Isn't it convenient that God built-in a weight loss and sobriety plan into the liturgical calendar?"

Self-control, as I've seen it practiced, is often motivated by self-contempt. I don't like myself. I'm too fat. I drink too much. I never exercise.

And so let me offer you a word – if this is your version of self control, you are far afoot from anything St. Paul imagines.

Look at the words that surround it in the passage above - *love, joy, peace, patience, kindness, generosity, faithfulness, gentleness.* Do these sound like burdensome products of rigid, self-contemptuous discipline? Of course not. These are the heart-responses of one whose life is so utterly rooted in Jesus that gentleness simply emerges, kindness overflows, peace lingers.

The true self in Christ is our inner orchestral conductor, and the orchestra players are every part of us still fighting, still vying for control, still seeking transformation. Self-control is our joyful, gentle, and faithful work of inviting every anxious part of us, every angry part of us, every resistant part of us to relax its grip and find compassion in Christ.

---

Prayer:

*Good and Gentle God, your sense of control is never demanding and always inviting, never forced but always gifted. Your compassion teaches us the way of compassion toward ourselves and every one we encounter. Cultivate gentle, faithful, and joyful self-control in me, I pray. Amen*

## Saturday Week 2

*I pray that out of his glorious riches he may strengthen you with power through his Spirit in your inner being, so that Christ may dwell in your hearts through faith. And I pray that you, being rooted and established in love, may have power, together with all the Lord's holy people, to grasp how wide and long and high and deep is the love of Christ, and to know this love that surpasses knowledge—that you may be filled to the measure of all the fullness of God. Ephesians 3:16-19*

New words catch my eye every time I read this extraordinary passage, perhaps my favorite in all the New Testament. Today it was the word "rooted." At other times, "established." Sometimes a phrase – "long and high and deep is the love." There are untold treasures for you in multiple, slow readings of this text.

St. Paul is talking about something that happens in our "inner being." Not in our church. Not in our kids. Not in our relationship (though each of these things will draw the benefits). No, the image here is of Christ dwelling in our hearts. And the implication is that we will experience profound rootedness, power, community, and a love that surpasses anything St. Paul could explain in a letter.

At this point in the Lenten season it's likely that some of the original excitement about the prospect of this season for your growth has lost its fervor. You get busy. A Lenten devotional is put aside for more pressing matters. Maybe you've picked this up on a Saturday looking to salvage what's left. I'm not sure where you are, but it doesn't matter.

St. Paul's prayer is that *out of his glorious riches he may strengthen you.* Somehow, someway, God has a storehouse of grace for you and for me. Somehow, someway God knows that we need his grace to be strengthened. Could he know, right now, how busy and preoccupied you've been and still be gracious to you? Is that possible?

Do you hear God's longing for you in this passage? Can you give yourself the gift of multiple readings, perhaps even noting what words stir in you as you read? God longs for you to dwell in and live from your deepest self, rooted and established in him. He longs for you to fall into the goodness of "the fullness of God."

---

Prayer:

*God of glorious riches, strengthen me. Root me. Establish me. Dwell in me. Deepen your love in and through me, so that I might be a conduit of this love to all. Amen*

# WEEK 3
# IMAGINE THE KINGDOM

### Third Sunday in Lent

*Once Jesus was asked by the Pharisees when the kingdom of God was coming, and he answered, "The kingdom of God is not coming with things that can be observed; nor will they say, 'Look, here it is!' or 'There it is!' For, in fact, the kingdom of God is among you." Luke 17:20-21*

It is said that Leo Tolstoy wrote, "In the midst of winter, I find within me the invisible summer." I think this gets to what Jesus is saying in Luke 17.

The Kingdom is not something that can be manufactured, strategized, or packaged. It's not a brand. It's not a possession. It can't be bought and sold, built or torn down. In other words, this Kingdom which comes with the reign of Jesus is the antithesis of our controlling, managing, and editing ego.

Perhaps this is why these words are spoken to the Pharisees. In that day, there was no better representative of a manufactured, managed and manipulated kingdom than the Pharisaical version of it.

This is why Jesus could playfully say, "Tear it down! I'll rebuild it in three days."

Sometimes, for me, to be "in the Kingdom" requires me only to close my eyes. It's winter outside – when my eyes are open – but it's summer when I close them. If, amidst silence, the inner voices can dim and the pressure to do something can relax, a sense of peace ensues. Sometimes I'll say, "Jesus is that you?" And I'll imagine him saying, "Yes, I'm here. I haven't gone anywhere. I'm always with you."

Granted, this is an exercise of the imagination. And yes, I'm trusting the good old Story to be true – that Jesus has come in-the-flesh, has died, has risen, and has sent his life-giving Spirit to dwell in me.

I'm believing a bit of that old Belinda Carlisle song too, I suppose -

> Oooh baby do you know what that's worth
> Oooh heaven is a place on earth.

Heaven is a place on earth. God dwells among humans – you and me. No, heaven isn't "up there" somewhere. It's not located somewhere between Venus and Saturn. God came. Emmanuel dwelled with us. His Spirit dwells in the church and in our hearts. Heaven is, quite literally, within you.

The old sages and mystics knew this. Some people live like it today. Because paradise is literally a breath away, they can close their eyes and imagine. These folks don't waste a whole lot of time buying boats and fur coats.

One of my favorite mystics of all – St. Teresa of Avila – wrote about this heavenly place in you and me. She called her work *The Interior Castle* and she imagined a mansion fit for a king, a beautiful place where intimacy with God is privileged over anything else. A favorite translator of mine wrote an introduction to her work describing this inner mansion like this:

> There is a secret place. A radiant sanctuary. As real as your own kitchen. More real than that. Constructed of the purest elements. Overflowing with the ten thousand beautiful things. Worlds within worlds. Forests, rivers. Velvet coverlets thrown over featherbeds, fountains bubbling beneath a canopy of stars. Bountiful forests, universal libraries. A wine cellar offering an intoxication so sweet you will never be sober again. A clarity so complete you will never again forget.[13]

Will you imagine this Kingdom with me in this Lenten week? And will you dare imagine that God's Kingdom is among and within you?

———————

Prayer:

*King Jesus, you've come near, more than I can imagine. Or can I? Have I even tried? I commit to imagining this extraordinary reality – that your heaven is more near than I think, that your paradise is within and among me. Give me the eyes to see what is already here and now. Amen*

### Third Monday in Lent

*In those days John the Baptist appeared in the wilderness of Judea, proclaiming, "Repent, for the kingdom of heaven has come near." Matthew 3:1-2*

"All I heard was repent-repent-repent growing up," my 25 year old friend said. I was probably 30 at the time, and wanting to be relevant and edgy I said, "I hate that word, too. It just conveys to people that they're bad."

I hope I didn't steer her too far afoot. You see, I get the visceral and painful response to the word based on her fundamentalist background, but nevertheless I'd tell her today that, indeed, she must repent.

Yet, in a way she hasn't yet imagined…

Imagine the Kingdom in our midst. Paradise here and now. Freedom for captives. Food for the poor. Homes for refugees. Infinite delights in the mystic sweet communion discovered in contemplative silence. Who wouldn't want to repent?

Repentance is a tricky word. While it's been used in tragic and abusive ways, it is quite a simple word picture – *turn around*. If I were to say, "Hey kids, Disney World is near – turn around!" it's a safe bet they would. That's exactly what John the Baptist is doing here.

Turn around! Well that requires attending to where you're going right now. And I will venture a guess that, like me, you're trying to find heaven in a romantic relationship, paradise in an all-night binge, security in a lottery ticket. Where are you turned towards? What has captured your imagination?

The reality of God-dwelling-within is this: we are often turned to the periphery of our lives, and not to the center. King Jesus is home on his throne, waiting like the patient father for you and for me – prodigals that we are – to turn around. The infinitely patient God is no further from you than the heart beating in your chest, and yet you've tried to find him in a chocolate donut, a one-night stand, a shiny new car.

I'm not trying to guilt you. If you're feeling it, though, it might be an opportune time to ask this question – what was I really looking for? Believe me, Jesus isn't waiting to scold you, he's waiting to embrace you. But he can't receive you if you're not looking.

Recently, someone I've been spiritually directing said to me, "Chuck, it feels like when I tune into the reality that God dwells within me more close to me than I am to myself, my whole body vibrates with an energy that feels better than anything I've ever known." I believe the Bible calls this "delight." And it was a word frequently on the lips of the Psalmists, early church theologians, medieval mystics, Puritan contemplatives, traditional hymn writers, and always little children – who have that stunning capacity to see beauty and goodness where the rest of us don't.

Repent, for the kingdom is near. Turn around. Take a look. Exercise a bit of your sanctified imagination. What goodness might you find and fall in to if you dared to look?

---

Prayer:

*God in whom I delight, I want to taste and see a sweetness and a beauty in you that I look for in a thousand other places. I realize you're not looking to scold me for looking elsewhere – you're just longing for me. I believe! Help my unbelief! Amen*

## Third Tuesday in Lent

*Abide in me as I abide in you. Just as the branch cannot bear fruit by itself unless it abides in the vine, neither can you unless you abide in me. John 15:4*

Abide.

What a strange word. I don't use it much. Do you?

Some Bible translators use the word "remain." Remain in me. But that sounds off to me - sort of like "you must remain here until the officer says you can go."

Abide.

When all else fails, when I've done my Greek studies and consulted my lexicons and bored my wife and daughters with questions about their observations, I go to my pastor-translator, Eugene Peterson. His books on life, and particularly pastoral life, have formed and shaped me. His Bible translation (some might not like that term!) brings new insights and surfaces some of the original flavor of the first writers. Peterson's translation goes like this:

*Live in me. Make your home in me just as I do in you.*

Whoa. That hits home, quite literally.

The great St. Augustine once said, "God is more near to me than I am to myself."[14] He called God our "homeland." If the Bible, Peterson, and Augustine are right and God is "home" in us, then I've got a confession to make: I'm not home.

It's actually kind of like this: I live somewhere in the backyard. In fact, it's not even a comfortable place. It's a tent on the hard cold ground. And, even more, I don't even look at my home very often. I've got lots of other distractions to keep my attention. And sometimes, I even begin to think damp tent is as good as it gets.

God is at home but I am away. Can you relate? Imagine living on the grounds of a palatial estate, but never entering the doors. Imagine peeking through the windows but never living within. Franciscan priest Richard Rohr says, "We cannot attain the presence of God because we are already totally in the presence of God. What's absent is awareness."[15]

Jesus says, Make your home in me just as I've made mine in you.

Abide in me as I abide in you.

And then…remain there! The distractions aren't nearly as satisfying.

---

Prayer:

*Abiding God, I long to be at home in you and you in me. That you are far closer to me than I realize is a mystery, but one that captivates my distracted mind. Would you patiently but intentionally pursue me, invite me, and never, ever give up, even when I look away? Amen*

## Third Wednesday in Lent

*Do not let your hearts be troubled. Believe in God, believe also in me. In my Father's house there are many dwelling places. If it were not so, would I have told you that I go to prepare a place for you? John 14:1-2*

The disciples of Jesus were desperately fearful that Jesus was leaving them. And I can tell you – in twenty years of pastoring and counseling, I've talked to plenty of women and men who feel like God is as far away as Mars.

In my church, we proclaim the Apostle's Creed almost every Sunday. One of the proclamations we make is this: Jesus ascended into heaven. And, as the popular misunderstanding goes, he went to build a heavenly palace for us to dwell in when we, in the end, rise like ghosts into the sky.

Heaven is not a far-away place, however. Heaven is another dimension, more near to us than we realize. Respected New Testament scholar and Episcopal Bishop N.T. Wright says, "The ascension of Jesus…is his going, not way beyond the stars, but into *this* space, *this* dimension."[16] We use language that conveys a "going" but it is not a going *away*, it is a going *deeper*. Again, we've got to exercise holy imaginations to see and experience this.

C.S. Lewis imagines this process in a way I can relate to. He says that our home needs some significant repairs. God's mansion-building project requires an extreme makeover. Perhaps you, like me, like to watch HGTV sometimes, and appreciate the transformation that happens when imaginative designers meet skilled laborers. Jesus has entered into this new, deeper heavenly dimension to do his grand re-design, his extreme makeover of you and me and the entire cosmos. He is one with the Creator, after all! C.S. Lewis writes, "You thought you were going to be made into a decent little cottage: but He is building a palace."[17]

Lent is often a time for spiritual touch-ups. Some use this liturgical season to "get right with God," to "recommit to reading the Bible," to "develop healthier spiritual habits." When I hear this, I sense that people are still operating from the old, pre-Jesus script that the Pharisees were working off of, the one that I imagine to be a re-painting of the outside of the house while the inside rots. This is why Jesus called the Pharisees "white-washed tombs."

No, stretch your imagination a bit further. The King is building a palace. And the King has sent his Spirit to begin the work in you, from the inside-out. You – God's living temple – are a top priority in God's Kingdom restoration project. You, with all of your baggage. You, with that history of abuse. You, with the failed attempts to overcome that addiction. You, with your squeaky clean outside. You, with your doubts about it all. God is far more committed to you than you are to yourself, if you can imagine it.

And so, let the work begin. Surrender to it. Partner in it. Fall into the goodness God has for you.

---

Prayer:

*Ascended Jesus, I'm trying to imagine that you are not far away, but actually present to me in a way that doesn't make sense to my analytical mind. But nothing is impossible with you. And so, would you do the work of re-creating me from the inside out to be the beautiful mansion you long to dwell in? Amen*

## Third Thursday in Lent

*The Lamb at the center of the throne will be their shepherd, and he will guide them to springs of the water of life, and God will wipe away every tear from their eyes. Revelation 7:17*

Always water. Waters to pass through on the exodus journey. Waters to plunge into on our baptismal journey. Waters to cleanse. Waters to purify. Waters to quench thirst. Jesus as "living water." And "streams of living water" flowing from within those in whom the Spirit dwells. The River of Life in the new heavens and new earth.

Always water.

Jesus calls those who are blessed "thirsty for righteousness." Wet tears stream from those who longings go unsatisfied. It would seem that our very bodies are living demonstrations of our organic connection to water. Indeed, 60% of the human body is water!

Always water.

As I write, I'm mindful right now that while I was in the frigid frozen tundra of Michigan yesterday, I sit today poolside in Phoenix, AZ where in my line of sight a large, stony bridge pours forth gallons of glistening water into a sky blue pool. The water meanders through a series of rocky canals above, winding down until it passes over a time-eroded curved edge, plunging ten feet into the waters below. And then, what was above and what was below are one.

Augustinian monk and Villanova professor Martin Laird writes, "We might liken the depths of the human to the sponge in the ocean. The sponge looks without and sees ocean; it looks within and sees ocean. The sponge is immersed in what at the same time flows through it."[18] When I consider Laird's words, I think of what my friend Jason said on a retreat I led not long ago. He said, "I experience God when my body descends into the water, when I am suspended in it. That's what it is like to be in Christ."

The water descends from the stony waterfall above and then it plunges into the depths, becoming one with the expansive waters below. The Spirit plunges as streams of living water into our very being washing and cleansing and purifying and enlivening and refreshing in ways our baptism promised. Our tears are joined with these waters, our lives entangled with God's life.

And the Lamb guides us here, says St. John. To the struggling churches he writes his apocalyptic letter as a message of comfort and imaginative vision. The Lamb – slain and risen – is both the guide and the Living Water, the forgiving victim and the refreshing stream. In the final chapter of his vision, St. John writes, "Let anyone who wishes take the water of life as a gift."

If I'm honest, I seek to be joined with many different things. I look for connection and oneness in a thousand different places. I long for the living waters, but look in empty wells.

But for a moment now as I peer ahead at the plunging waters, I long to fall into the goodness of God. How about you?

———————

Prayer:

*Living Water, you refresh and cleanse and purify and heal. You long to wash over me in a flowing fountain of grace and peace. And I long to plunge into your depths. May I fall into the refreshing goodness of your Oneness. Amen*

### Third Friday in Lent

*For as I went through the city and looked carefully at the objects of your worship, I found among them an altar with the inscription, 'To an unknown god.' What therefore you worship as unknown, this I proclaim to you. The God who made the world and everything in it, he who is Lord of heaven and earth, does not live in shrines made by human hands, nor is he served by human hands, as though he needed anything, since he himself gives to all mortals life and breath and all things. From one ancestor he made all nations to inhabit the whole earth, and he allotted the times of their existence and the boundaries of the places where they would live, so that they would search for God and perhaps grope for him and find him—though indeed he is not far from each one of us. For 'In him we live and move and have our being'; as even some of your own poets have said,*

*'For we too are his offspring.*

*Acts 17:23-28*

One of the reasons I call myself a follower of Jesus is because I believe, deep down in my soul, that he is the very center of the story of the world. All our hopes and aspirations are tied up in Jesus, who reveals who God really is.

And people hunger for life he offers. You do. I do. We see the hunger in insatiable appetites for instant intimacy, constant connection, lasting love. St. Paul says that people are searching, hoping they might "grope for him and find him." In spiritual practices of every tradition, people are groping. In fad diets and body makeovers, people are reaching for him. And St. Paul even uses a pagan poet to show the hunger.

*In him we live and move and have our being. We are his offspring.*

Even the pagan poets intuited a fundamental union with the divine. And if they do, perhaps your neighbor does. Or your co-worker. Or your yoga teacher. Or your son who has left Christian faith to 'explore'. Perhaps God is more near to all of us than we think. Could we exercise that kind of imagination?

I've heard dozens of stories from missionaries who ventured into tribal territories to evangelize a pagan people only to discover that when they told the Story and named Jesus, the response was,

"Oh yes, we know this story well." St. Paul says it himself in Romans 1. God has revealed enough for everyone to grope for it, albeit frustratingly at times. At a deep down, intuitive level, each and every one of us knows. But we seem to be adept at settling and sabotaging, choosing substitutes that satisfy for a moment but don't last. Even those who claim Christian faith go about living and moving and being in other places.

Of course, if you follow Paul in Romans, he's not terribly optimistic about a life that doesn't find its center in Jesus. In fact, you might just say that it will becoming a 'living hell." We all know the life – the one the prodigal son chose, fun as it was for a time, which eventually ended in a pig pen. I've taken the turn a hundred times, and still do, as I give way to distracting and hopeless substitutes for the real life Jesus offers. But St. Paul is also pretty quick to caution all of us, especially those who think they've found it and own the territory, to withhold judgment of others. In fact, have you experienced what I've experienced? Have you noticed that some who don't claim Christian faith seem more deeply connected to the Divine than many of us "Christians" are? As a lifelong Christian 'insider' this makes me a bit squeamish.

The great Jewish theologian Abraham Heschel once said that we fail to understand God "not because we aren't able to extend our concepts far enough but because we don't know how to begin close enough."[19] Faith becomes a head trip. Christianity is a series of box checks - you're in or out based on your right answers. And yet, having received theological degrees and having served as an ordained minister, I spent many years living out of union, speaking the name of Jesus but not at all at "home" in him. I didn't start close enough. I began in my head, not in my deepest being.

Perhaps, instead of determining insiders and outsiders, we ought to leave the details up to God and simply abide. Perhaps, instead of condemning those who don't agree, we ought to wade gently into the waters of curious conversations, sharing our longings, our desires, our intuitions of a life of deep and divine connection. Some of my favorite conversations are with those who don't (yet) claim Jesus but intuit a profound divine connection.

With seemingly lavish grace St. Paul says, "to those who by patiently doing good seek for glory and honor and immortality, he will give eternal life." And so, my imagination grows into patient exploration, hopeful that the God in whom each and every human being lives and moves and has their being will reveal the central character of the Story in vivid color, Jesus, who satisfies every desire.

———————

Prayer:

*Ever-present God, give me the eyes to see and the ears to hear of your goodness in everything you've made. Give me the capacity to see a hunger for you in each and every person I meet. And may Jesus satisfy every desire of ours. Amen*

## Third Saturday in Lent

*As you, Father, are in me and I am in you, may they also be in us, so that the world may believe that you have sent me. The glory that you have given me I have given them, so that they may be one, as we are one, I in them and you in me, that they may become completely one, so that the world may know that you have sent me and have loved them even as you have loved me. John 17*

I wonder if we believe this. I wonder if we believe that Jesus longs for us to be one in him, and with one another. I wonder if we can even fathom God's "glory" in Christ being given to us. Can we imagine the kingdom coming in such a personal, relational way?

In a world of selfishness and competition, it's hard to grasp the idea that the maker of heaven and earth would be so utterly unselfish.

In my family, we battle about who will take a shower first and how much hot water we'll have and who gets to be in the bathroom and for how long. In our workplaces, we look over our shoulders, wondering if our colleague might get the promotion ahead of us. We live a world where people battle over profit, feed on the idol of accumulation, wage wars over who possesses what.

And yet, from the very beginning it seems that the very nature of God is selfless, giving infinitely of his infinite resources, continually overflowing in Love. For St. John, Love is God's very character (1 John 4:8). God's been trying to give away the greatest gift of all since the beginning of time, but we're masters of sabotage, trying to bottle up our own versions of transcendence and love and glory when infinite Love is offered freely.

But what strikes me about St. John's imagination in this passage more than anything else today is this: *that the world may know*. God's very best advertisement, to put it crassly, is our embodiment of his love. It's not the most effective mission strategy. It's not the buttoned up theological argument. It's not the most emotionally moving worship experience. It's Love, embodied in women and men, young and old, rich and poor, have's and have nots, people of every tribe and nation.

Sometimes in Lent I'll get very focused on me – my growth, my sanctification process. But it struck me when I was taking Communion at church recently that the Table we approached was the great equalizer, that streams of people would come forward to receive who didn't share the same blood or net worth or ethnic background or political beliefs all to participate in the life of Jesus. I watched and I wondered – do we even know what's happening right now? I lamented about how ritualistic the sacrament had become for me and so many.

God longs to give away his glory. Love, freely given, is available in infinite proportion. What if we, in becoming one with Jesus, became one with each other, and in this showed a watching world how beautiful the community of God can be?

———————

Prayer:

*Loving God, open my heart to both receive and give, to drink deeply of your Love and then to give abundantly from it. Too many times I've settled for something less, and too often our world chooses a much less satisfying pathway to the Love it needs. Open our imaginations to see you giving of yourself, infinitely, not just for our sakes but so the world may know. Amen*

# WEEK 4

## TAKE THE HUMBLE PATH

### Fourth Sunday in Lent

*When Jesus saw the crowds, he went up the mountain; and after he sat down, his disciples came to him. Then he began to speak, and taught them, saying: "Blessed are the poor in spirit, for theirs is the kingdom of heaven." Matthew 5:1-3*

Blessed are the poor in spirit. Of all the things Jesus could start with, this is it?

Imagine this: Jesus had just gathered his young disciples, teenage young men that they were, for their very first lesson. Just prior to this, they'd been with Jesus among the "crowds," with a broad ethnic mix of women and men from Galilee, Decapolis, Jerusalem, Judea, and beyond the Jordan. The attention was fixed on this miracle worker, Jesus, who seemed to be able to heal every disease, even giving hope to epileptics and paralytics and demoniacs. Can you imagine the buzz?

To be a teenage follower of Jesus in this eclectic crowd! Social media would have been abuzz. How special must these young followers have felt? And then, with seeming ignorance to the opportunity a large crowd was for a preacher, Jesus says, "Let's get out of here." And he takes a much smaller crew of followers up a hillside to chat with them about what the kingdom of God really means.

*Blessed are the poor in spirit, for theirs is the kingdom of heaven.*

What a buzzkill, Jesus! Just think of it – these newly empowered young followers who are feeling quite special about themselves now told that the first principle of this new kingdom order is poverty! What could Jesus mean?

He wasn't telling them to sell off their stocks and IRA's – no, he was saying something far more radical. To a group of young, newly empowered, feeling-kind-of-special followers he was saying, "You must come to the very end of yourselves."

20th century poet T.S. Eliot in his beautiful "East Coker" imagines a path through a world that offers only fragile, temporal solutions. Amidst war and secularism and cheap versions of progress, Eliot imagines another way, an inward journey:

> We must be still and still moving
> Into another intensity
> For a further union, a deeper communion
> Through the dark cold and the empty desolation,
> The wave cry, the wind cry, the vast waters
> Of the petrel and the porpoise. In my end is my beginning.[20]

Jesus is envisioning us falling into the goodness of his kingdom. It's not a journey that requires us to climb a ladder up into the divine heights. No, this kingdom of heaven requires us to let go, to fall, to come to our end. The heavenly dimension available and accessible to all is not up there, but as close as your body, as close as the ground you stand on.

The Beatitudes of Matthew 5 will be a hard message for these young followers. After all, when you're young it's all about the upwardly mobile life. We accumulate degrees and edit resumes and iron our best shirts for the big interview. We're always striving for the next promotion, the big payday. For young followers looking for a Messiah to give them titles and riches and glory, this message might just be a hard one to swallow. Maybe they, and all of us, need a bit of time to sit with it. In the next Beatitude, Jesus will invite us to grieve, too.

For Jesus, the Lenten journey must go through a Cross. For each of us, there is a daily dying in which every part of us that grasps, accumulates, and strives chooses, once and for all, to surrender. This is a lifetime work. It's not slow, it's not easy, it's not sexy. In time, our true selves in Christ emerge from the ruins like the resurrected Jesus, freed to live the full, abundant life -- the heavenly life -- Jesus promises. But a lot of dying needs to happen. Every resistant part of us is invited to surrender.

Sit with this difficult invitation from Jesus today. There is no need to hear it as a command to sell all your possessions immediately and wallow in guilt about the life you've lived. That's not the point! Jesus is inviting us to freedom, not guilt. He's showing us the way to goodness, not guiltiness. He's offering the opportunity to remove every obstacle to union. As we sit with Jesus and consider this, will we take the journey?

---

Prayer:

*Lord Jesus, you open a way to us that seems daunting but is ultimately freeing. And yet, it's hard to comprehend. What does it mean for me? And how can I live for you in a world that lives to consume, possess and accumulate? Give me wisdom, and be my guide. Amen*


## Fourth Monday in Lent

*Blessed are those who mourn, for they will be comforted. Matthew 5:4*

Years ago I wrote a book called *Leaving Egypt: Finding God in the Wilderness Places*. It narrates our stories through the story of the Exodus from Egypt, an 11 day journey that took forty years. In other words, it took a day for Israel to leave Egypt, but forty years to get the "Egypt" out of Israel. It always seems to take a lot longer for us to leave what's behind and claim what's ahead.

There is often a conflict within me about this. Parts of me want to journey ahead, growing into the person I long to be. Other parts of me resist, still craving the attachments of my past. In the mix, the voice of my true self can get squelched. I can feel lost, stuck, even sad amidst the cacophony of competing voices within me.

Part of my resistance is that I don't want to say goodbye. I like those old parts of me quite a bit. Some have served me well. I hid behind humor and words early in my life, but it got my somewhere. Part of me was a driven workhorse, and that helped my career. It feels kind of sad saying goodbye – like, I'm saying goodbye to parts of me that served me well, parts of me that knew how to have a good time, parts of me that could outwork the next guy.

There is a grief in this process, isn't there? When Jesus imagines us coming to the end of ourselves, he's imagining the death of every little self, every "old self" as St. Paul might say, every false self, even the ones that served us well. I imagine parts of me still in Egypt, still addicted to certain ways of being and living and working that must be freed from their slavery, even if they come kicking and screaming. I imagine an inner conversation with that busy workhorse part of me who reminds me that he's done the hard work of helping build my career, advance along the way, even write books. But I also imagine Jesus whispering, "Can you rest now and let me lead?"

My wife said recently that she's seen me change over the years. I used to be a whole lot more anxious and obsessive than I am today. What's interesting is that there were parts of the old me that she liked (as well as parts she is glad to see growing up.) Truth be told, the couple that fell in love 22 years ago has seen a lot of dying along the way. And with that process, there have been tears of sadness and joy.

Jesus wasn't trying to play therapist to the disciples when he challenged them to mourn. He was recognizing the reality of switching stories, of transitioning from a life geared toward their own self-fulfillment to a kingdom-life, with all it entails. The next years for those sitting at his feet on that hillside will be tougher than they know. They've chosen to enter into a new Story, led by a new (true) self, freed to live and love and serve and even die.

What must you mourn as you leave the old behind? It's quite alright to like, even to love, old memories, old attachments, old parts of you from the past. But it may also be time to thank them and to say goodbye, to grieve and mourn their loss. The new lies ahead.

---

Prayer:

*Suffering Servant, you knew pain and were well-acquainted with grief. In becoming one of us, you've shown such great love and solidarity with our journeys, as well. Thank you for giving me permission to grieve. I know that it is only through tears that I will see your kingdom with new eyes. Amen*

### Fourth Tuesday in Lent

*Blessed are the meek, for they will inherit the earth. Matthew 5:5*

I have a favorite poem called "The Self Slaved" by Patrick Cavanaugh. It's too long to quote the entire poem here – go google it – but there are several lines that are powerful:

Me I will throw away.
Me sufficient for the day
The sticky self that clings
Adhesions on the wings
To love and adventure...

I will have love, have love
From anything made of
And a life with a shapely form
With gaiety and charm
And capable of receiving
With grace the grace of living
And wild moments too
Self when freed from you.[21]

What is stunning to me about this poem is how humble it is. The writer, Patrick Kavanagh, has obviously come to a point in life where he's tired of the old, "self-righteous" and "sufficient" self, the self that thinks it knows where it's going and how to get there. He's obviously lived long enough to grow tired of the self which is incapable of the "grace of living," longing now even more deeply for the life of freedom, full of "wild moments," "capable of receiving," capable of love.

Every maturing life must go through periods of humiliation, where our egos are shown their limitations. Inheriting the earth is not about attaining, accumulating, or conquering. You don't get the life you want by buying it. Joy can't be bottled. Those who are "meek" have been refined, through brokenheartedness and grief, now humbled and freed from self-necessity. They inherit the earth because they've fallen into the goodness of it.

When I share this in a talk, a small quarter of the room nods with a knowing look while many sit and stare, unsure of what I'm getting at. We're so addicted to upward mobility that the thought of necessary humiliations along the way is puzzling. Maybe a story will help. I was speaking with an Uber driver recently who had great success in his first 35 years of life in Silicon Valley. And then, out of the blue, he received an invitation from his board to meet. With details of his narcissistic, self-serving behavior, the board gave him 30 minutes to clear the office he'd occupied for 3 years, a bare bones "go-away" financial package, and an apology for not doing it sooner. It was swift, shocking, and painful. He was red-faced, heartbroken, and enraged. He fought back over the next weeks until his mind and body literally couldn't fight any longer. He told me that he surrendered on that day.

Driving for Uber to pay the bills in the city he once viewed from a 20 story office was the ultimate humiliation. At times, he'd pick up people who once adored him. But he was humbled. He was no longer looking for someone to blame, no longer playing the victim. In a 30 minute drive from my hotel to the airport, I experienced the free soul of a man who'd descended from the heights, quite literally, and fallen into goodness. He said to me, "Every ride is now an opportunity to learn, to share, to be thankful for every moment."

Blessed are the meek. They've found their way down to the ground, to the place where Jesus is and where Jesus can meet them.

--------

Prayer:

*Humble Savior, you paved the way for my journey of downward mobility. But I'm scared. Sometimes, this feels like too much. How much of me needs to die? How does that even happen? Will you walk with me on the way and guide me into places of growth, even when I resist? And will I really experience goodness? Will you be near, even in my questions? Amen*

## Fourth Wednesday in Lent

*Blessed are those who hunger and thirst for righteousness, for they will be filled.*
*Matthew 5:6*

When I was a kid, our house was Grand Central Station for my neighborhood friends. This meant that lots of snacks and drinks were necessary. After a couple of hours of pickup basketball or football, we'd bring our massive hunger and thirst into my kitchen in a frenzied rush. Perhaps you can imagine the ravenous hunger of a bunch of middle school boys.

Now, can you imagine how hungry and thirsty the Jewish people were for a Rescuer after hundreds of years of exile? Can you imagine the excitement as the gossip spread – "He's here, he's really here. The Messiah has come! We're free!" And can you grasp the shock of the young followers assembled on that hillside when Jesus announced that the kingdom come was not the end of their hunger and thirst, but an invitation to it?

Blessed are the broken. Blessed are the mourners. Blessed are the meek. And now this? Perhaps, you can relate. Maybe you're one of those folks who've been following Jesus for years, and yet the marriage hasn't gotten better, the depression hasn't diminished, the economic issues haven't subsided. Or maybe you're a new follower of Jesus, and you hoped that faith would bring sweeping changes in every area of your life. But, your heart still aches.

We are a people in search of fulfillment. If the Garden of Eden story teaches us anything, it teaches us that we're not even content with paradise. There is always something more. We now know that each year millions of dollars are spent on psychological research to determine what you and I hunger for, and that marketers use this research to custom-tailor ads that will stir longing in us. The General

Motors research division once called this "the organized creation of dissatisfaction."[22]

Interestingly, Jesus doesn't satisfy every hunger and thirst when he comes. But he doesn't mock them either. He ennobles them. Hunger and thirst define the kingdom dweller, the Jesus-follower. Holy desire animates us. And for what? *Righteousness* – the world set right again, hearts re-tuned, painful relationships restored, the self-righteous redeemed, racism razed. Jesus invites us into a deeper hunger and thirst, beyond better wifi signals and a better coffee shop in our neighborhood.

The first four beatitudes chip away at our cheap versions of happiness, exposing our Garden-grown propensity for self-fulfillment, and inviting us downward, back to the ground of our being. But notice – they don't invite us into a prude and squeamish guilt-and-shame based existence. No, this downward journey is the way of life, and life to the full.

Lent, as I said in the Acknowledgments, is from the old English word Lencten, the "springtime" of the soul. Out of death, life. Out of a thawing soil, green. Days lengthening. Sun warming. Hope growing. But for this life-giving process to happen, each season must be embraced and honored for its redeeming work. Yes, even the winter's dying.

And so, in this Lenten season as we straddle death and life, enter in. Let the broken-mourning-meek-hungering vision of the kingdom do its deep, soul-transforming work on you. Fall into the goodness of God's beatitude vision.

---

Prayer:

*Risen Christ, we hunger for the same righteousness you long for, but if we're honest we're often satisfied by smaller things. We thirst for justice in our broken world, but sometimes settle for quick fixes. Stir a deeper hunger and thirst for your kingdom and your righteousness. Amen*

## Fourth Thursday in Lent

*Blessed are the merciful, for they will receive mercy. Matthew 5:7*

"I'm blessed with the gift of mercy," she said to me, with a twinkle of eagerness in her eye. You got the sense that she was ready to jump into any ministry I asked her to do. And there were needs at the church…plenty of them. I needed her. But, I told her no.

Why would I do that? I knew her too well to draw her in to something that could further intensify a wound in her. You see, she had learned a long time ago to give as a way of getting. She grew up an only child in a family of high achieving parents, and she got their attention by being the child-without-needs, the child always ready to come through for Mom and Dad. Her room was spotless. Her grades were high. And she never whined or complained. As her pastor, I could not ask her to serve without having a long and hard conversation about her life and my vision for her growth.

The quality of mercy Jesus imagines here is different than eager giving. The merciful person – because she's a broken, lamenting, humbled, and longing soul – is close to the ground. She's fallen into goodness herself. And from that place, she gives freely, with no strings attached.

In pastoral ministry, I've meet many eager givers. I've seen them come through the seminary as well. And we often bless their supposed gifts. But too many today help from a place of woundedness. And this form of helping often leads to resentment and emptiness.

When I think about how and why I give, it's complicated. I give to bless. But I also give to be thanked. I give to be noticed. I give to feel special. I give to satisfy an appetite for usefulness. I give to stay busy. I give to get benefits. I give from a whole host of troubling and complicated motives.

The question for each of us is this: Are we on the beatitude journey of Jesus? If we are, we're doing the deep archaeological dig in our souls necessary for authentically merciful giving. And when we are close to the ground of our own being, close to that humus-soil of meekness, we are prone to meet others right where they are, as wounded-healers to weary and broken souls.

We all long to be rescuers, at some level. We long to be heroic. But sometimes our rescuing masks our own core needs for love and security. Jesus makes a far better Rescuer than you and me. As we're humbled and as our sense of self-importance slowly dissipates, we might actually find ourselves eager to participate as mercy-givers, not because we're fishing for satisfaction but because we're longing to see the world made right.

---

Prayer:

*Rescuing Savior, I realize now that you are a far better "rescuer" than I am. In fact, in rescuing another I may not recognize that it is I who most desperately need rescuing. Continue to do the work of humbling me for participation in your kingdom life. I really do long to be a mercy-giver. Amen*

### Fourth Friday in Lent

*Blessed are the pure in heart, for they will see God. Matthew 5:8*

What bugs you the most about Christians? You can ask this question to longtime Christians or new ones, skeptical seekers or ardent atheists, and you'll likely get a similar answer: *hypocrisy*.

You know it. You've experienced it. You've likely practiced it. It comes from a Greek word that means "play-acting." It's about stage craft – playing a role on the outside, but not living it from your whole being. And Jesus was fairly merciless when it came to hypocrites. Matthew 23 is a *tour de force* against the hypocritical religious:

> *"Woe to you, scribes and Pharisees, hypocrites! For you tithe mint, dill, and cummin, and have neglected the weightier matters of the law: justice and mercy and faith. It is these you ought to have practiced without neglecting the others. You blind guides! You strain out a gnat but swallow a camel! "Woe to you, scribes and Pharisees, hypocrites! For you clean the outside of the cup and of the plate, but inside they are full of greed and self-indulgence. You blind Pharisee! First clean the inside of the cup, so that the outside also may become clean. "Woe to you, scribes and Pharisees, hypocrites! For you are like whitewashed tombs, which on the outside look beautiful, but inside they are full of the bones of the dead and of all kinds of filth. So you also on the outside look righteous to others, but inside you are full of hypocrisy and lawlessness. Matthew 23:23-28*

On the other hand, Jesus has a vision for wholeheartedness. It emerges in the one who comes to the end of herself, mourns the old, is humbled by the process, and grows in new longings for a life of grace and mercy. This person is pure of heart.

No, not squeaky clean. No, not ready to be sainted. No, not adorned with a halo. No, not perfect. *Pure.*

"She is a person of character of character consistency, a person who rings true whenever you tap her. She keeps promises," says one theologian.[23] What you see is what you get. The inside matches the outside. There is no show.

Words like purity, and even perfection, get thrown around a lot in Christian circles, and some of us even believe that God expects nothing less than this gold standard of morality. We become adept at climbing the ladder of holiness up to God with our Lenten fasts and our daily disciplines only to realize that the holy top of the mountain is unattainable. And even more, Jesus isn't there! He's come to us.

In fact, we've really distorted both words – purity and perfection. Each in their own way actually get at what I've called wholeheartedness.[24] This is an experience of oneness and worthiness in Christ. It is that "abiding" we mused on days ago, that being-at-home in Jesus.

And this, you'll be shocked to hear, comes not from climbing but falling – falling into grace, falling into goodness, falling into your life. "God comes to you disguised as your life," as Paula D'Arcy says. And that means that God comes in and through the concreteness of your very being – who you are, where you are. Christ's dying and Christ's rising takes place in you. You may actually begin to believe that God isn't 'out there' residing somewhere between Jupiter and Venus, but within.

The so-called hypocrites can't stand this kind of talk. God must be attained, achieved, arrived at. God is a goal, attained by checking the boxes. Any talk of God's beautiful intimacy in Christ sounds blasphemous.

And yet, it's the true story we're so blessed to participate in. God comes so near that he changes you, even you, from the inside out. He's not afraid of what's in you, and if it takes a lifetime he'll work to remind you that shouldn't be either. The God-in-you reality should remind us every day that it's not about cleaning up our act for God, but making our whole being available for God's abiding.

God's doing the cleanup work in your right now. You can resist or surrender. You can fool around with the externals or fall into his infinite goodness, always available to you, right now and forever. You can close your eyes to grace or open them in order to "see God," who is more near than you are to yourself.

---------------

Prayer:

*God-in-us, you're not afraid of what's inside me. Why should I be afraid? You are making me new, cleaning me, purifying me, making your home in me. Housecleaning has never been so glorious. Give me the eyes to see. Amen*

## Fourth Saturday in Lent

*Blessed are the peacemakers, for they will be called children of God. Blessed are those who are persecuted for righteousness' sake, for theirs is the kingdom of heaven. Blessed are you when people revile you and persecute you and utter all kinds of evil against you falsely on my account. Rejoice and be glad, for your reward is great in heaven, for in the same way they persecuted the prophets who were before you. Matthew 5:9*

"I'm a peacekeeper," she said to me, with her head tilted downward. I had asked her if she could speak to her boss about sexist and racist remarks he'd made toward her. But she made clear that it was not her personality to stir the pot.

"What if you could become a peace*maker*?" I asked. She looked confused. I wondered aloud with her whether or not it was time for someone to declare *shalom* where there was no peace.

"But I might lose my job!" she retorted.

She'd been there for 10 years. She was the senior engineer in a Silicon Valley startup, and at 35 she was probably more than a decade older than most of her colleagues. Her boss and the founder was 32, a young, brash, and narcissistic guy who experienced his early success as a sign of impenetrability.

I could conceive of several different ways in which she could and should tackle racist and sexist comments, but peacekeeping wasn't on the list. After running through options which included outside, legal intervention, she said to me, "I've been here with him a long time. I think I owe it to him relationally to say something clearly and directly." Wow. Something new was emerging in her.

We walked through her language and tone. She wanted to practice – to imagine herself in the conversation, speaking non-reactively but with strength. I coached her to share how it felt and what she needed. We talked about specific requests she'd make. She did meditation exercises in which she imagined speaking to him, in the setting they'd gather, face to face, with clear speech and direct eye contact. She wisely planned for another senior employee to be present. And then the big day came.

When she called me that evening, I could hardly wait to hear what happened. My formerly anxious and diminutive client had chosen to become a peace*maker*. She knew the risk. She'd planned for multiple contingencies. She'd also received the affirmation of several peers at work who were willing to go to battle if and when it was necessary. However, she'd go before them.

I can't imagine anything more Christ-like, in some respects. But I worried whether or not I was unwittingly setting her up to "cast her pearls before swine." Regardless, she'd made the choice after a lot of deliberation. She didn't have to do this. She longed to. Something in her shifted in our weeks of discernment. She was beginning to have a vision for a workplace where people wouldn't walk on eggshells, where trust and vulnerability could fuel creativity and innovation. Her imagination was lifted to a place of wholeness and vitality.

"Well, it was disastrous," she said, with an unexpected calm. "Within minutes he was twisting my words into some conspiratorial theory about me undermining him for years. Within the hour, the board was contacted, my desk was cleared, and I'm now sitting at home with a glass of wine and a box of memories a decade old."

I was stunned. Of course, I felt responsible to some degree. I didn't say a word.

"And I feel exhilarated," she said. "I don't think I've ever felt more alive than I did today. The texts I've received range from profound gratitude to words like 'hero' and 'role model.'" While her own future was uncertain, she anticipated a larger fight in which she'd play some role in and for the sake of her colleagues that remained.

Flocks of people did not come to Jesus that day. A narcissistic founder did not fall to his knees and pray the Sinner's Prayer. No, but something profound happened. Words of *shalom* entered into a dark space. A light shined in the darkness. A woman experienced persecution. A courageous soul experienced rejoicing. And the kingdom was among us.

I think that this brave woman's imitation-of-Christ happens every day. She's not going to be sainted. Her name won't appear on some wall of courage in downtown San Francisco. But her words brought disruption, holy disruption into unholiness. And she felt alive.

You'd probably like to hear the end of the story. I would too. But like many biblical parables, it is unresolved. Like our lives, it is unresolved. I don't live in San Francisco anymore. I've heard an update or two. She's landed on her feet. He's still doing his narcissistic thing. But I believe the kingdom came in a tangible way on that day, through an ordinary woman, much like you and me. She certainly inspired me to follow Christ on the path of humility.

———————

Prayer:

*Peacemaking God, every day you go before us. But it takes a lot of courage for me to step into the fray. I'll admit, I am kind of scared. But I also long to be alive, to live with freedom. Give me the courage to live for you. Amen*

# WEEK 5

# WRESTLE WITH GOD

## Fifth Sunday in Lent

*For my sighing comes instead of my bread,*
*    and my groanings are poured out like water.*
*For the thing that I fear comes upon me,*
*    and what I dread befalls me.*
*I am not at ease, nor am I quiet;*
*    I have no rest, but trouble comes.*

*Job 3:24-26*

In a culture where we've become experts in pain avoidance, wrestle with God. In a world where self-help books promise quick fixes, enter the boxing ring. In a society that wipes away tears before they've fully been shed, embrace your pain.

But what does that mean? For Job, at least, it meant wrestling with God until he came to a place of silence, of surrender. Dogged by so-called friends who were trying to theologize his experience, friends who were trying to find some rationale, Job just kept wrestling. Challenged by accusations, Job kept wrestling. Job kept wrestling until his arms could no longer grip, until his hands opened in a posture of surrender.

Some have tried to find a secret recipe for understanding God in this 42 chapter, 12 round boxing match called "The Book of Job." But you can't find it. It's not there. There's no "how-to" of pain management. No, this book is a heavyweight bout. Job enters the ring. He looks pain square in the eye. And he knows that he can't do that without looking God square in the eye.

Lent is a Job-like season. It's a time when we pay attention to our strategies of avoidance. It's a season in which we rip off our band aids and do the major heart surgery necessary to discover how we sabotage the God-abiding life. It's a season in which we acknowledge our propensity to avoid the ground of our being and the limitations of our creaturely life.

And pain holds the possibility of returning us back to that ground. When tragedy affects us, there is no more room for pretense. When health is stolen from us, our false selves relax their controlling grip. All of a sudden we're thrown into a raw, unfiltered space. We're thrust into the boxing ring , and it feels like God is our greatest enemy.

In these times, the fluff has to go. Throw out the self-help book. Refuse the Kleenex meant to clean you up quickly. Avert your eyes when the super-spiritual comforter comes with her encouraging Bible verse. Let your entire being descend into its earthy, rugged ground. "Speak what you feel, not what you ought to say."[25]

Remember, blessed are the broken. On the wilderness journey of life, there is no path around, under, or over – only through. Don't waste your time trying to figure it all out. Go through it, with boxing gloves on, honest as you can.

Maybe, in the end, you'll be able to surrender with Job. Maybe in the wordless ground of your being, connected again to your creation-dust, you'll be able to say with Job

*I'm convinced: You can do anything and everything. Nothing and no one can upset your plans. Job 42:1*

---

Prayer:

*God, I'd like to enter into a more honest place with you. In the midst of a world that sanitizes suffering, I want to be a person who has nothing to hide between us. Give me the courage to trust you with my whole heart and story. Amen*

## Fifth Monday in Lent

*I do not understand my own actions. For I do not do what I want, but I do the very thing I hate. For I delight in the law of God in my inmost self, but I see in my members another law at war with the law of my mind, making me captive to the law of sin that dwells in my members. Wretched man that I am! Who will rescue me from this body of death? Romans 7:15; 22-24*

"I just don't get myself," he said. "I don't understand why I keep returning to this addiction. I'm done. I'm just done."

He was bent over in a posture of pain I'd never seen on him. If you were there with me, you'd like feel too that he was at some kind of breaking point. I believed him when he said he was done.

He'd been in counseling on and off for years with a variety of qualified clinicians. The therapeutic work traversed all of the important and necessary channels – his past, his family system, generational addictive patterns, and more. He had figured a lot out. He could name abusive patterns and dysfunctional relationships. But his addiction continued to raise its ugly head.

What I've seen is that no matter how much 'figuring-out' we do, whether therapeutically or theologically or otherwise, change remains elusive. You can know a whole lot about your past and still remain chained to it. This man remained in chains despite thousands of dollars of therapy.

I might not need to convince you that St. Paul was a pretty good theologian. In fact, I'm returning to a part of this passage used earlier in this book because it's so helpful. But passages like this, while helpful in constructing a theology of sin or law or humanity, are lost to us if we don't feel the weighty struggle Paul is facing. Do you sense his anguish? Can you hear him wrestling?

I've deliberately left out vs. 25 because I don't want you to miss the struggle. You can look it up on your own time. But I'll give you a hint: Paul's wrestling leads him to Jesus. Yet, he doesn't get to Jesus without the wrestling. He doesn't get to Easter except through the sufferings.

My addicted friend hadn't yet hit his gracious and generous bottom yet. He was an answer-seeker. He devoured therapy and theology. He longed to know the intricacies of the human struggle. But he did it all in his head. He was a consumer of information, but not a participant in transformation.

Participation involves wrestling. And that's a messy business. As tears began to pour from his eyes, he looked at me as if he was coming undone. But in truth, he was falling into goodness.

Prayer:

*Gracious God, that you would meet me where I am is a gift. I am often afraid of my sin and brokenness, but you are not. Allow me to bring every part of me to you honestly. Amen*

## Fifth Tuesday in Lent

*When he opened the fifth seal, I saw under the altar the souls of those who had been slaughtered for the word of God and for the testimony they had given; they cried out with a loud voice, "Sovereign Lord, holy and true, how long will it be before you judge and avenge our blood on the inhabitants of the earth?' Revelation 6:9-10*

How long, oh Lord? This is an ancient cry. It's a cry of Psalmists and wisdom writers and prophets. But in a surprising New Testament twist, the cry of lament is found on the lips of those martyrs who've already gone to be with the Lord.

Lament in heaven? I've heard a bunch of funeral sermons, but I've never heard one emphasizing the sadness of those who've gone to be with Christ. What can this mean?

What it means is this: *How long?* is a cry for us all. It's a cry for those at the bottom of the pit and those at the loftiest heights. It's a cry for the poor and for the rich. It's a cry for the abuse victim and for the ecstastic new mother.

You see, these are wrestling words. These are words for a world in which injustice still lingers, where racism dehumanizes, where pornography toxifies. They are words for a world in which Christians are still martyred, innocent children are aborted, and women are paid less than men. There is always an opportunity to cry out *How long?*

We live in a world longing for shalom, groaning for redemption (Rom. 8). Things are not the way they're supposed to be. Some of us ignore this. Others cope with cynicism or with denial or with distraction. But Lent invites us to pay attention, not merely to our ordinary problems – credit card debt or the need for weight loss – but to the more complex and messy ones. Lent invites us to wrestle on behalf of anyone, anywhere, who needs the justice and mercy of Christ.

A pastor was once over-heard saying, "Lent is kind of like a God-sanctioned self-improvement project." When I heard this, I cringed. No, Lent isn't about a bit of cleaning up and repair work but about personal and cosmic transformation. As we're changed, our cries become the cries of the world. We join our voices with the heavenly voices who see a world not yet set right.

The agenda of my old selves is always (false) self-centered. My true self in Christ, however, joins in union with the One who came near to love to join and even weep with those who long for mercy and justice. Prayer, then, can become a wrestling on behalf of the Palestinian Christian denied human rights, the pastor's wife being emotionally abused by her narcissistic husband, and the teenage girl raped by her boyfriend now wondering how to end her pregnancy.

To become participants in this cosmic wrestling match requires us to do some Lenten soul-work, however. We've got to attend to patterns of denial, avoidance, and distraction. We've got to name the false realities we live into that mask the real. We've got to open ourselves to the groaning of the entire creation, not just our own.

But, this isn't an invitation to a depressing life! As our hearts become more expansive, joy grows within us. We see through the pain into the profound goodness of others made in the image of God. We join with Jesus, who makes his home in me and you and every broken imager-bearer.

So, join your voice to the saints who've already gone before us. *How long?* is a prayer for all of us.

---

Prayer:

*Justice-and-Mercy seeking God, you hear the groans of your creation and your children. I want to join my 'How Long?' to theirs. I long to wrestle on behalf of others. Stir in me a heart for those who need this cry. Amen*

## Fifth Wednesday in Lent

*Jacob was left alone; and a man wrestled with him until daybreak. When the man saw that he did not prevail against Jacob, he struck him on the hip socket; and Jacob's hip was put out of joint as he wrestled with him. Then he said, "Let me go, for the day is breaking." But Jacob said, "I will not let you go, unless you bless me.' So he said to him, "What is your name?" And he said, "Jacob.' Then the man said, "You shall no longer be called Jacob, but Israel, for you have striven with God and with humans, and have prevailed." Gen. 22:24-28*

"It feels like my struggle is just a revelation of how little faith I have," she said, battling to look me in the eyes. Her shame was palpable. She'd heard it time and again – real Christians with real faith see real victory in their lives.

She pinned her Facebook wall with optimistic quotes and positive thoughts, but these were only a mask. Somehow, she hoped that by portraying positivity, she'd become positive herself.

How strange is it, then, that so many women and men in Scripture seem to wrestle? In this passage, Jacob himself seems to be wrestling with this "God-man" – one who seems to be close enough to be intimately engaged and yet powerful enough to re-name him.

He was once called Jacob. Jacob, which could mean "followed" or "supplanted," becomes Israel, "one who struggles with God." The one who was clasping at Esau's heel is now the one who stands toe to toe with God, who enters the boxing ring with God, who is wounded by God.

From now on, an entire nation is defined by his wrestling match with God. The people of "Israel" have a vocation embedded in their name.

I once heard a theologian say that one of Israel's major problems in the Old Testament was that it actually failed to wrestle well with God. Instead of wrestling, she went back to old habits and loves, old idols and addictions. Instead of wrestling, she'd look for security in military power and human leaders. But where she failed in her vocation as God-wrestler, Jesus didn't. Jesus accomplishes what Israel failed at.

And because we are "in Christ" – because Christ is more near to us than we are to ourselves – we, too, become God-wrestlers. We, too, are marked not by a merit badge but by a limp. Christians make Jesus known not in strength but in weakness. Christians are transformed not by climbing the ladder but by wrestling in the ring, where we're always close to the ground.

You see, once again our limits are on display, and it's quite alright with God. The limp isn't a disqualifier. The struggle isn't a strikeout. Falling to the mat isn't our end. In fact, our very wrestling is a declaration of trust. By grabbing hold of God by the arms and wrestling, we're declaring our desires, our longings, our hopes. We're declaring that God is real – not some ghost-like figure but One who enters in.

Those who follow Jesus are the "new Israel," with a new identity, a new vocation, a new mission. Our wrestling is not just for ourselves, but for the sake of all. I wonder what it would be like for a watching world to see us wrestling honestly with God, unafraid of our limp, engaged relentlessly with a God who is more near and available than we can imagine!

———————

Prayer:

*Wrestling God, I've got to admit – it's hard to imagine getting in the boxing ring with you. The story of Jacob seems like an old fable, not a relevant invitation. But I want to live out my vocation and mission as the God-struggler, for my sake and for the sake of the world. Amen*

## Fifth Thursday in Lent

*Vanity of vanities, says the Teacher, vanity of vanities! All is vanity. All things are wearisome; more than one can express; the eye is not satisfied with seeing, or the ear filled with hearing. Ecclesiastes 1:2;8*

Everything is vanity. Fleeting. Like trying to catch the wind. Now you see it, now you don't. An exercise in futility.

God is there. God is not there.

"I believe. Help my unbelief" (Mark 9:24).

Can you relate? The ongoing tug-of-war in my soul leaves me wondering whether or not I'm really a follower of Jesus, at times. I am fickle – I find myself in church worshipping, but just as quickly I am even more engrossed in a high-budget action movie that awakens my senses. At other times I'll be sitting with a client I'm counseling engrossed in her story with a sense that God is bigger than I've ever known. But shortly after I'll see another whose gruesome story of abuse makes me wonder how God can be both good and all-powerful.

The one who wrestles with God also wrestles with doubt. It is inevitable. Read the Psalms alone and you're in for a wild ride through the land of doubt, uncertainty, and despair. In fact, if you pay attention to the many biblical dialogues between God and humans – kings, prophets, ordinary folks – you'll see instance after instance of "Are you sure, God?"

In fact, when I look at the Scriptures as a whole, I'm reminded that God didn't provide a recipe book or an owner's manual. The Bible is Story, through and through, chock full of human expressions of every imaginable emotion. God is not some diagnosably Obsessive Compulsive Disorder list-maker, not some insecure taskmaster. In fact, in trusting us with the Bible in its cacophonous beauty, he seems to be demonstrating how very secure he is in his own being with our doubts, disputes, and despair. Maybe God is more of a grown up than I thought?

The great 16th century theologian and reformer John Calvin once wrote, "Surely we cannot imagine any certainty that is not tinged with doubt, or any assurance that is not assailed by some anxiety."[26] Any certainty, John? Really? But yes, it's comforting to know that all of my supposed certainties may be laced with doubt, assailed by anxiety. It's comforting to know that God is secure even amidst my insecurity.

This is why God is not just comfortable with but delights in being more near to us than we are to ourselves. God is not afraid of you. God is not afraid of your doubts. God is not afraid of your anxiety. Perhaps the reason "Do not fear" is so often on God's lips is because he is ultimately fearless when it comes to us. God's own trust in us is absolutely tied to his confidence in his own love and care for us.

And so wrestle with each and every doubt. Speak it plainly. Share it with confidence. God is secure, and God is a much better listener than anyone you've ever known.

Prayer:

*Powerful and Good God, knowing that you are secure helps me to feel a bit more secure. Knowing that you are willing to hear my every doubt frees me up to express to you concerns that I thought were weak and selfish. I want honesty in every part of me. Give me the confidence to trust you. Amen*

## Fifth Friday in Lent

*My eyes are spent with weeping;*
  *my stomach churns;*
*my bile is poured out on the ground*
  *because of the destruction of my people,*
*because infants and babes faint*
  *in the streets of the city.*

*Lamentations 2:11*

I've performed many more weddings than funerals. I've had the privilege of officiating ceremonies in Napa Valley, CA and Paris, France, at the foot of the Grand Tetons and the belly of a cruise ship. Each memory stirs feelings of joy and newness, hope and promise.

I also live as a white male with a PhD, some resources, a beautiful family, and a now tenured faculty position. Life is good. So it's hard to relate, at times, to texts like the one above. I'm not living at the epicenter of Middle East terrorism or inner city violence. I don't see the destruction of bodies on my streets and I've can't relate to my black friend's regular racist interactions with his neighbors in our town.

But can I open my eyes? Can I *choose* to see, to listen to stories, to step into places of discomfort, to enter in to the pain?

I've had the privilege of being a therapist, among other hats I wear. That has been my place of entrance, of companionship, of alliance. It's in that place that my blinders come off and I'm invited into the solidarity of another's story. But it's hard, at times – really hard. I'd rather not believe that church-going Christians are racists, that seemingly good men are narcissistic abusers, that sweet grandmothers can be sexual predators. I *choose* to enter in. I choose to see, however painful the truth and the stories are.

Where do you enter in? If Lent is a season of repentance, at least a part of that repentance is choosing to move toward the pain. Beyond personal maturation and transformation, Lent is a season of participation in the sufferings of the world, something we're called to do (Philip. 3). Just as we choose to remove every fig-leaved and false-selved mask, we choose to dive beneath the societal mask of supposed exceptionalism and freedom and prosperity to see the world's deep pain. We choose to see.

Our true self in Christ has a kind of homing beacon. It's compass-direction leads us to our central vocation – love of God and love of neighbor. The true self is guided by compassion, kindness, love, and empathy. It moves toward every so-called "other." It refuses to categorize, demonize, or diminish the image-bearing humanity of another. But I often live out of every other agenda-driven false self within. I've got work to do. And so do you.

When we read the stories of Scripture, including the difficult laments like the one above, our blinders are removed. In Scripture, we do not find a sanitary tale of ascent into heavenly bliss, but an often messy and painful fall into the goodness of God's creation. Through the messy stories of Scripture, we watch beauty emerge from brokenness, redemption from despair, freedom from slavery. But we've got to look, perhaps with fresh new eyes, in order to see the pain.

And so, wrestle with God's word. And wrestle with the implications of living in this beautiful-and-broken world. Where might you choose to enter in?

I've done a lot of weddings. I like hope and new beginnings. I like happy stories and hopeful promises. I want to celebrate goodness wherever it is found. But I'm also learning that it is found in the unexpected and sometimes messy places, too.

––––––––––

Prayer:

*Incarnate Christ, you moved close to the pain of the world. You entered in. You became a bearer of that pain for the sake of the world. I want to follow you into the beauty and brokenness of this world for the sake of its transformation…and mine. Amen*

### Fifth Saturday in Lent

*Then he took the twelve aside and said to them, "See, we are going up to Jerusalem, and everything that is written about the Son of Man by the prophets will be accomplished. For he will be handed over to the Gentiles; and he will be mocked and insulted and spat upon. After they have flogged him, they will kill him, and on the third day he will rise again.' But they understood nothing about all these things; in fact, what he said was hidden from them, and they did not grasp what was said. Luke 18:31-34*

Luke says it pretty clearly here: They didn't have a clue. Of course, he puts it more politely: *They did not grasp what was said.* But it's devastating, nevertheless. On the cusp of the most weighty, significant, monumental week in history, the disciples didn't get it.

How, after three years together, did they miss it?

How, after three years together, were they clueless?

No matter our proximity to Jesus, it seems that we're often blinded by our alternative agendas for God. Even those closest to him missed the clues he was laying along the way. And who could blame them – does anyone have a category for God-in-the-flesh dying and rising?

God's destroy. God's conquer. God's battle each other. They punish their rebellious slaves. They don't mysteriously appear in-the-flesh on a redeem-and-restore mission that involves becoming the victim, the slain Lamb.

Do we get it today? We have all kinds of alternative agendas for God. We call God into action like the warrior gods of old for the sake of our supposedly righteous causes. But God's action in Christ unravels our alternative agendas for God. He beats the sword into a plowshare (Joel 3:10), making peace through his willingly surrendered life.

Wrestle with that. Because, if we're honest, we hardly believe it today. Our alternative agendas for God often look like the old-fashioned agenda. We pray to God for the success, the victory, the win. Our prayers are shaped like ATM-withdrawals to a God who takes sides, so we assume, rather than a God who suffers and dies so that we'd no longer need to take sides.

The next week is a week to wrestle with the reality that this God, who came in-the-flesh, came even closer in the Spirit. This surrendering and sacrificing God took up residence in us, through the Spirit, in order to reconnect us to our original and beautiful humanity, in order for us to become Christ to others. Somehow, someway, we've got the wrestle with this hard reality – the baton of Jesus is passed to us. We bear his life and (dare we think it) his death. If you read St. Paul's letters carefully, this theme takes center stage.

I've come to think of this last-week-of-Lent wrestling match as an opportunity to die alongside Jesus, as a chance to identify every obstacle to union with him. I want to not only believe but experience St. Augustine's profound statement – "God is more intimate to me than I am to myself." I want to run through the streets with Catherine of Genoa as she exclaims, "My deepest me is God!" I want my inner life to be transformed to such a degree that I really can grasp it, that I really have a clue, that I'm really tuned in to the surrendered journey of Jesus. I want to fall, with Jesus, into the goodness of redemption. Won't you join me?

_____

Prayer:

*Lamb of God, remove every obstacle to union. I long to be one with you in spirit, in desire, in purpose. It is with this hope that I enter Holy Week. Amen*

# WEEK 6

## FOLLOW JESUS

### Sunday of the Passion: Palm Sunday

*Tell the daughter of Zion,*
*Look, your king is coming to you,*
*humble, and mounted on a donkey,*
*and on a colt, the foal of a donkey.*

*Matthew 21:5*

The journey began with these words: *You are dust and to dust you shall return.* If you recall, these are words of beauty and goodness, words that invite you back into your original creatureliness, your inherent limitations, the ground of your being – your "enoughness" as God's imager-bearer.

You may recall, also, that our journey has taken us into the in-the-flesh life of Jesus, who became human, who took on human limitations without regret. Jesus – so committed to you that from the very beginning he's been searching you out, coming for you, eager to redeem and restore, to dwell with you and in you, by the Spirit.

Can you follow this Jesus? He's not driving a BMW. He's not accompanied by the Secret Service. He's not dressed in his Sunday best.

Can you follow this Jesus? He's not a king like other kings.

Can you follow this Jesus? He doesn't care how impressed you are.

In those days, to follow someone was to become more like that person, to embody their character and virtue, their teachings and actions. For three years the disciples followed Jesus, but if you check their record it's full of infighting and comparison. That's because following someone like Jesus is a lifelong, intentional, transformational, and (need I say it again!) often painful process.

We become what we follow. And so who do you follow? What do you follow? Where are your habits being formed? And are you open to going in a new direction, following the One who will take you places you never dared explore?

If I'm honest, I'm not sure. I mean, what will it cost? I've got a life to live and bills to pay and daughters to send to college. I want to sell books and be admired. I want the appearance of following, but not the cost.

But here is the gratifying goodness of it all – to become more like Jesus is to become more ourselves. Thomas Merton wrote, "To be born again is not to become somebody else but to become ourselves."[27] All this talk of dying to ourselves is not some morbid form of self-negation. No, it's ultimately generative and life-producing. The seed must fall to the ground and die in order to live. We must die to every other version of our-selves to become ourselves.

You see, our lives are caught up in a much larger dynamic. Our stories are best seen in and through a much larger story of union with Jesus and our sabotage of it. James Finley says it well:

> On the one hand there is the great truth that from the first moment of my existence the deepest dimension of my life is that I am made by God for union with himself. The deepest dimension of my identity as a human person is that I share in God's own life both now and in eternity in a relationship of untold intimacy. On the other hand, my own daily experience impresses upon me the painful truth that my heart has listened to the serpent instead of to God. There is something in me that puts on fig leaves of concealment, kills my brother, builds towers of confusion, and brings cosmic chaos upon the earth. There is something in me that loves darkness rather than light, that rejects God and thereby rejects my own deepest reality as a human person made in the image and likeness of God.[28]

Following Jesus on this journey, in one sense, is an affirmation of your own deepest reality as one made in God's image. It is about finding yourself, not in some strange self-fulfillment sort of way, but in union with the life of this surrendering King.

In this week, we seek to follow Jesus.

———————

Prayer:

*King Jesus, your journey is simultaneously exciting and frightening for me. It seems as if it comes with a cost. But at the same time, the thought of "becoming myself" wholly in you is something that stirs my heart. Draw me further and deeper into this union and communion, I pray. Amen*

## Monday in Holy Week

*Here is my servant, whom I uphold,*
  *my chosen, in whom my soul delights;*
*I have put my spirit upon him;*
  *he will bring forth justice to the nations.*
*He will not cry or lift up his voice,*
  *or make it heard in the street;*
*a bruised reed he will not break,*
  *and a dimly burning wick he will not quench;*
  *he will faithfully bring forth justice.*
*He will not grow faint or be crushed*
  *until he has established justice in the earth;*
  *and the coastlands wait for his teaching.*

*Isa. 42:1-4*

He is coming to bring *justice*. Don't let that word scare you. It's not the apocalyptic horror story people make it out to be. No, God's justice is about setting everything aright, restoring the world's brokenness, making all things new, including you.

But the old imagery is helpful, at times. You know – the imagery of fire and brimstone, the imagery of wars and floods. You see, justice isn't always pretty. God's setting-things-right comes not with flowers laid down on the path before us but on a trail of tears. Cosmic and personal transformation doesn't look like paying for a spray tan in order to change your image. It's a dying and rising. It's bloody.

"Cut out your eye if it causes you to sin," Jesus says. That's bloody. Of course, we don't go around cutting people's eyes out to make a point. But maybe you get the spirit behind it. Jesus is saying – Do the hard work. Do the heart surgery. Transformation isn't easy. It's a bloody mess.

Like Jill. That's not her real name, but she's a real person. She was terrorized by a physical, emotional, and spiritual abuser for decades. When I met her, she was soulless. She had no desires, no passions, no needs of her own. She was practically mute save for the parroting of her husband's opinions. She was radically out of touch with her *self* – that beautiful image-bearing self in Jesus. The self she was wearing was a tattered and beaten one, a persona built over the course of many years through much childhood neglect and trauma. This was the only garment she wore.

Jill's dying-to-rising journey might not make the annals of the saints. She didn't journey to a foreign country and save thousands of souls. No, she had no life to give for another, no self to offer. We had to find her lost self first. This took many, many months. She feared having her own opinions, expressing her own needs. But as she did, something grew within her. I saw her smile. She asked for a cup of coffee. She decided to start exercising. And her tyrant husband became enraged.

Jill endured brutal abuse during those months to the point of leaving her husband. She stuck around longer than I wanted her to. But when she left, it was *her* leaving. She'd grown weary of those old garments. She longed to be dressed in the new clothes of Jesus. She claimed Ezekiel 16 as her story:

> *I clothed you with embroidered cloth and with sandals of fine leather; I bound you in fine linen and covered you with rich fabric. I adorned you with ornaments: I put bracelets on your arms, a chain on your neck, a ring on your nose, earrings in your ears, and a beautiful crown upon your head. Ezekiel 16:10-12*

Despite apocalyptic drama and profound abuse, she longed to bear the beauty of her divine image, and desired to become a blessing to others.

His lawyer was a warrior. He threatened her. He threatened me. For months she stepped in and out of her new identity, sometimes falling back into the fearful doormat-of-a-wife burdened by guilt and shame. Justice for Jill was not easy. Her desire to follow Jesus meant walking the gauntlet of crucifixion, to her old self, to her destructive marriage, to a church community that wouldn't support her, to his financial security. She kept walking though.

Christ is coming to bring justice. And if we follow, we may find ourselves walking the bloody path, too. Transformation always involves a dying. In Jill's case, the death to her old self came at a high cost but became an extraordinary metamorphosis.

During our last session together, we celebrated the emergence of the butterfly from the transformative chrysalis. Jill would go on to become an extraordinary champion of other women like her longing to follow Jesus to freedom. This is the kind of justice Jesus is bringing in concrete ways, not necessarily for the annals of the saints, but extraordinary nonetheless.

---

Prayer:

*Just King, we long for justice in the big crises and in our smaller stories, in the lives of broken people and in a groaning creation. We long to become our new selves in Christ, transformed in order to be a blessing to others. May it be so. Amen*

## Tuesday in Holy Week

*The hour has come for the Son of Man to be glorified. Very truly, I tell you, unless a grain of wheat falls into the earth and dies, it remains just a single grain; but if it dies, it bears much fruit. Those who love their life lose it, and those who hate their life in this world will keep it for eternal life. Whoever serves me must follow me, and where I am, there will my servant be also. Whoever serves me, the Father will honor. John 12:23-26*

Jesus will be there with you. Right there with you. Before you and behind you. To your left and to your right. At your head and at your feet. In your inmost being. Jesus will be right there with you.

He says, *Whoever serves me must follow me, and where I am, there will my servant be also.* He will be there.

We follow Jesus like a grain that falls to the ground and dies. We follow Jesus to the ground, to our ground.

Like my student in a MA in Counseling program who I was assigned to supervise. He thought he had entered to get the skills necessary to help others in need. But he didn't realize he was in need. I recall the evening when he was counseling an addict on the verge of losing his marriage. I was watching through one of those mirrored windows. I watched him stumble through the counseling session, trying to offer bits of advice that were not landing. We debriefed afterwards and I offered a hard truth:

"John, you're that man," I said with a compassionate seriousness. He stared at me blankly. "You've been trying to fix your own broken life with some duct tape here and some gauze bandages there, but it's worse than you think, isn't it?"

His head dropped, and tears began to flow. Soon enough, the dam broke, and he was crying out, "I'm hurting so much. It hurts so bad." I wrapped my arms around his back and held him for 10 minutes.

The grain of wheat dropped into the earth that evening. He followed Jesus to his ground. He watered it with his tears. And the dying continued for the next months. But what began to emerge was beautiful goodness. Compassion – for himself and for others. Patience. Humility.

I watched as his entire posture changed with his clients. Gone were the quick fixes and in was empathy. His own tears flowed as he sat in hard places with clients.

I think that he is one of those who Jesus refers to when he says *Whoever serves me, the Father will honor.*

The grain that falls to the earth falls into goodness.

———————

Prayer:

*Humble Savior, I follow you on the path that leads into the earth, into what feels like dying but ultimately transforms. I follow you. Amen*

## Wednesday in Holy Week

*After saying this Jesus was troubled in spirit, and declared, "Very truly, I tell you, one of you will betray me.' The disciples looked at one another, uncertain of whom he was speaking. John 13:21-22*

Betrayal stings. It sends a singe of shame to the soul's depths. It prompts us to question everyone and everything. It shatters trust. It plunges the soul into a panicked tailspin.

Jesus was fully human, full of emotion – confusion, sadness, shame, anger, joy, ecstasy, contentment. How must this betrayal have felt? How did he not turn over the table in rage?

One of his closest confidantes cut a deal with the other side. With the Evil One, no less. Judas was a friend he walked alongside on long journeys – from Jerusalem to Galilee and back for a full 240 miles – and several times, I believe. I imagine that there were dozens of conversations during unhurried moments. Storytelling. Laughter. Breaking bread.

I'd kick him out immediately. But no, Jesus set the table. He invited his betrayer to the table. He broke bread with him yet again. In a strange act of hospitality, Jesus served his betrayer.

To follow Jesus is to enter in to the matrix of relationship. It is to move toward others with vulnerability. It is to show empathy. It is to give and receive. In a world calloused by relational wounds, closed off to intimacy, and clamoring for cheap imitations, Jesus paves the way for risky, vulnerable intimacy. Jesus risks it all – even betrayal – to fulfill his sacred vocation.

Last year a person I'd been counseling took a bold step into truth in her closest relationships. She named toxic and dysfunctional patterns that threatened shalom in her family, including her father's alcoholism and rage. She did all of this in the name of Jesus and for the sake of integrity. Within days, her father – the family's patriarch – told everyone in the family to cut her off. Social media connections were severed. Phone messages and texts went unreturned. To return, she faced the choice of forfeiting her integrity. She has been betrayed by her closest ones.

However, she continued to follow Jesus. In time, a new community emerged for her, marked by Christ-like humility, giving and receiving, justice-seeking, peacemaking, and vulnerable relationship. This became her new family. And though filled with grief, she continues to walk toward the Cross. The devastating episode returned her to the earth, to her ground, where like that grain of wheat she sat with tears until her anger turned toward compassion. She shared this note with me just a few weeks ago:

*Dear Family, I miss you. How I longed to see you at Thanksgiving. There was a fresh sense of grief as I thought about how you've cut me off. I want us to live in truth together, and if we cannot I will grieve some more. But know this – I have not cut you off. You are welcome at my table.*

———————

Prayer:

*Lamb of God, you do not cut me off. But sometimes I cut myself off from you. Sometimes I do this because I've felt the sting of betrayal, and struggle to trust. Mend my heart. Soften it. Allow me to open my table once again, even to my enemies. Amen*

## Maundy Thursday

*So if I, your Lord and Teacher, have washed your feet, you also ought to wash one another's feet. For I have set you an example, that you also should do as I have done to you. John 13:14-15*

She sat in my office, broken by a betrayal. I had no words. Her sense of her own dignity seemed shattered. I saw on her the face of one who feels worthless.

"I'll be right back," I said. I returned with a basin and water. "May I wash your feet?" I asked. She gave me permission, and wept as I gently washed them.

This was a true self moment, a moment when my deepest me in Jesus emerged to bless another. I was along for the ride. I'd never done this...and I've never done anything quite like it since. Maybe you've had the feeling too, the feeling of being connected to Love and getting out of the way long enough for Love to live through you.

Later that day, shame overcame me. Less selfless parts of me began to cry out, "That was a show. All for you and not for her. You're a phony." Another part of me chimed in, "She didn't deserve that from you. She's a mess. Let her deal with it herself." I was tossed to-and-fro in a torrent of inner fragmentation. A few moments later I exclaimed, "Stop."

It was like I was commanding the 'Legion' within. My inner world was in a frenzy, and I felt a bit like Jesus declaring to the raging waters, "Be still!" Over the next few moments I began tending to my various inner rivals, showing compassion to parts of me that needed care. As if I was washing the feet of ashamed and pained parts of me, I lavished them with care. Later that night, I fell into my bed in exhaustion.

Following Jesus means going to battle for the sake of the other. It means stepping into shame and confusion, pain and betrayal. It means alliance and advocacy, justice and mercy. But let's not forget we need the same ourselves. I'm convinced Evil wanted to sabotage divine dignity in me that day, and I'm grateful the Spirit stepped in.

Later Jesus would command, "Love one another as I have loved you." The word command is where we get the word 'Maundy' in Maundy Thursday. This is our command, our call, our vocation. We love because Jesus loves us. Jesus longs to show us compassion. Jesus knows the battle is hard, that we are weary, that sometimes it just feels like too much. He also knows our inner battles – the voices of shame and anger and self-contempt and avoidance and so many more. And so, through our True self in Christ, he becomes our servant, the one who washes our feet.

Can you imagine it? Jesus longs to wash your feet. He longs to show you the love he commands you to offer the other. On this day, why don't you practice receiving that love? Why don't you greet Jesus, at your very feet, touching the ground, a reminder once again that it is here that God reminds us who we are.

———————

Prayer:

*Humble Servant, you wash my feet! I can hardly fathom it. I never, ever feel like I do enough for you and for others. And yet you long to show me love.*

*You long to show me that in you, I am enough. Amazing love, how can it be! May I, too, be a blessing to others. Amen*


## Good Friday

*For he did not despise or abhor the affliction of the afflicted; he did not hide his face from me, but heard when I cried to him. The poor shall eat and be satisfied; those who seek him shall praise the LORD. May your hearts live forever! To him, indeed, shall all who sleep in the earth bow down; before him shall bow all who go down to the dust, and I shall live for him. Ps. 22: 24, 26, 29*

The road to Easter resurrection goes through Good Friday's dying. Every single transformative journey takes the same path. This is, at least in part, what Good Friday teaches us. We all must die. Like the grain of wheat, we must fall to the ground and die for new life to begin

Once again, the Psalmist reminds us that those who are truly surrendered go down to the dust. That's where we began at Ash Wednesday, and it's appropriate that this is where we approach our conclusion of the Lenten season, as well. The poor will eat. Those who return to the ground will bow. We don't see Jesus in the lofty heights but in the liminal spaces. Every human journey of transformation must take this downward path.

In fact, St. Paul takes it a step further. He calls our path a crucifixion. Paul says, "I have been crucified with Christ and it is no longer I who live, but it is Christ who lives in me. And the life I now live in the flesh I live by faith in the Son of God, who loved me and gave himself for me" (Ga. 2:20). He has been crucified? What does that even mean for you and for me?

It means that parts of us Paul calls "flesh" and many call "false self" must die. Each must go down into the ground, through the cruciform path, and be transformed. Self-sufficient and shame-based parts of me must die, and controlling and cavalier parts of me must die. My cruciform journey must touch every part of me – every not-yet-transformed part of me – until I become wholehearted, which I call the experience of oneness and worthiness in Christ.

The renowned British pastor and theologian John Stott helps me understand this when he writes:

> What we are (our self or personal identity) is partly the result of the Creation (the image of God), and partly the result of the fall (the image defaced). The self we are to deny, disown, and crucify is our fallen self, everything within us that is incompatible with Jesus Christ (hence Christ's command, 'let him deny himself and follow me'). The self we are to affirm and value is our created self, everything within us that is compatible with Jesus Christ (hence his statement that if we lose ourselves by self-denial we shall find ourselves). True self-denial (the denial of our false, fallen self) is not the road to self-destruction, but the road to self-discovery.[29]

This is our Lenten work, but this goes beyond Lent. This work continues through Eastertide and into Pentecost and throughout all of the seasons of the church year.

But this is delightful work. You see, all this talking of dying and cruciformity might sound negative and messy, but it's really about unshackling you from every idol and addiction and attachment that weighs you down. Truth is, life in the fleshy-false-self is enslaved life. It's unfulfilled life. It's burdensome life. It's momentarily-satisfying but soul-sucking life. It's non-life.

If John Stott is right, the new way through Good Friday leads to self-discovery, an opening of ourselves to becoming full known in Jesus. Remember when Adam and Eve hid. Now, we come out of hiding. We move toward vulnerability. We take the adventure of self-disclosure, the risk of intimacy. This is abundant life. This is freedom – naked and unashamed.

In a sense, it's what we've all been hungry for since the beginning. It's what the primeval story of Adam and Eve teaches us. We were made for more. And Good Friday is the ultimate gateway. Through our poverty, into the dust we go, trusting God's goodness to see us through into transformation.

---

Prayer:

*Crucified Lord, you died so that I might live. And you've paved the path for life, and life abundant, through the Cross. May I take this journey with courage and boldness, open to the transformative work you'll do in and through me. Thank you, Jesus. Amen*

## Holy Saturday

*Since therefore Christ suffered in the flesh, arm yourselves also with the same intention (for whoever has suffered in the flesh has finished with sin), so as to live for the rest of your earthly life no longer by human desires but by the will of God. 1 Peter 4:1*

David Tracy, a Roman Catholic theologian, has said, "There is never an *authentic* disclosure of truth which is not also transformative."[30] What he means, at least in part, is that the Christian claim on 'truth' is hollow if it remains a doctrinal claim apart from a lived experience of transformed lives. And, of course, Jesus places a big exclamation point on this when he calls himself "the way, the truth, the life." Indicting the religious experts, he shows truth by living it, by becoming our Passover, by going through hell to release us from our own hellish prisons. He shows us the truth by entering in, becoming a human being, into-the-dust of limitation and creatureliness in order to meet us right where we are. Jesus isn't a concept. No, Jesus lived a life and took a journey that is now ours to take.

As the sun descends beneath the horizon and darkness falls upon the earth, millions of Christians all over the world are celebrating the Resurrection-dawn at Easter Vigil services across the world. Darkness is required for a dawn. You cannot have authentic faith without it. Christianity is, in the end, no happy-clappy, health-and-wealth social club. It is about a transformed community, imaging the Son, walking the pascal way, dying and rising, resisting the violent-coercive-imperialistic way of consumerist culture, and most likely paying the price for it. Humiliation is not an option – it's an inevitability.

But the breaking dawn invites us to see that all is not doom and gloom. From darkness, the impossible is realized. With the disciples of Jesus scattered to the four winds, afraid to embrace a faith that might require *their* participation as those transformed by truth, Jesus emerges to a world that must now reckon with a very new reality. This new reality is that conflicts are not won and lost by power, intimidation, or violence. The real battle is won through self-surrender, humiliation, turning the other cheek, loving and blessing and forgiving our neighbor. The real transformation happens as every false self experiences death and resurrection within.

Jesus does not save us from suffering. He saves us from ourselves, which engages us in a process of profound transformation as every part of us that resists God is chipped and stripped away. And while this journey isn't as pretty as some would like it to be, it is real – a life lived awake and alert, a life lived vulnerably, a life lived with freedom. Read the great stories of the saints and martyrs. You will not find doom and gloom, but joy.

I long for joy. I long for my desires to match God's desires. I long to live in God's freedom. And – can I be honest? – when I'm simply indulging myself, I don't feel very free or joyful. When I've wasted a day living out of my avoidant self, when I've ruined a conversation living out of my cynical self, when I've exhausted myself living out of my achieving self, I'm not really joyful. I may get a laugh or some admiration, but I'm not joyful.

I want to end our journey together with an imaginative exercise which will nurture joy in these final hours of the cruciform night. On this Holy Saturday, I want you to imagine sitting very still in the midst of the darkness. The confusion of Good Friday has passed and the dawn of Easter has not yet emerged. All is quiet. We wait. We listen. All is still.

Can you hear your heart beating? Can you feel your feet on the ground? Can you feel the delight of not having to do a thing at all but sit still, rest, and be?

You've fallen into goodness. The goodness is the ground beneath you. The goodness is the dust to which you've returned. The goodness is your limitations. The goodness is the body God designed to be yours and yours alone. The goodness is the infinite presence of Jesus, by the Spirit, more near to you than you are to you. The goodness is the transformative work God is doing in the silence of your being without you even knowing it.

You sit here now in the dark with no one to impress, no one to please. In this place, you are simply enough, in Jesus. You are enough.

I want you to imagine every fig-leaved false self dissolving into oneness with Christ, centered in the very core of your being. Christ dwells in your innermost depths, welcoming you. Come. Relax. Enjoy. You are worthy. You are mine.

You hear the words with delight. In the darkness and in the stillness, all is well. Everything he has is yours. You are his beloved son, his beloved daughter. He sees you straight through to your core and smiles, delighting in his child.

You've fallen into goodness.

# ABOUT THE AUTHOR

Chuck has been married to Sara with 20+ years and has two teenage daughters, Emma and Maggie. He has authored three books: *Leaving Egypt: Finding God in the Wilderness Places* (Square Inch), *Toughest People to Love* (Eerdmans), and *Wholeheartedness* (Eerdmans). Chuck has pastored in two church plants, started two church-based counseling centers, and now serves as Professor of Counseling and Pastoral Care at Western Theological Seminary, Holland MI. He is also a Senior Fellow at Newbigin House of Studies, San Francisco and a church consultant. He holds a PhD in Psychology, a Master of Divinity, and a Master of Arts in Counseling, and is a licensed therapist.

[1] St. Teresa of Avila,

[2] Quoted in Curtis and Eldredge, *The Sacred Romance* (Nashville, TN: Thomas Nelson, 1997), p. 23.

[3] See Ch. 8 of my book *Wholeheartedness* for an elaboration of this psychological dynamic.

[4] Dietrich Bonhoeffer, *Dietrich Bonhoeffer Works, Vol. 8: Letters and Papers from Prison,* transl. Eberhard Bethge (Minneapolis, MN: Augsburg Fortress, 2009), pp. 221-222.

[5] See the works of Internal Family Systems theorist Richard Schwartz.

[6] St. Macarius, *Homilies* 15:32-33.

[7] Thomas Merton, *Conjectures of a Guilty Bystander* (New York, NY: Image, 1968), p. 155.

[8] See Richard Rohr, *Immortal Diamond* (San Francisco, CA: Jossey Bass, 2013), p. 5.

[9] See the work of Kristin Neff, University of Texas (Austin) researcher, including her book *Self Compassion.*

[10] St. Augustine, *Confessions* 10.27.38

[11] John Calvin, *Institutes of the Christian Religion,* III, vii, 6.

[12] Anita Barrows, *Rilke's Book of Hours: Love Poems to God* (New York, NY: Penguin, 2005), Kindle Locations 692-693.

[13] Mirabai Starr, *Teresa of Avila The Interior Castle* (New York, NY: Penguin, 2013), Kindle Locations 69-72.

[14] Augustine, *Confessions* 3.6.11

[15] Richard Rohr, *Everything Belongs* (New York, NY: Crossroad, 2003), p. 29.

[16] https://eerdword.com/2014/05/28/heaven-and-power-n-t-wright-on-jesus-ascension-part-1-of-2/

[17] C.S. Lewis, *Mere Christianity* (New York, NY: HarperCollins, 1980), p. 206.

[18] Martin Laird, *Into The Silent Land* (New York, NY: Oxford University Press, 2006), p. 17.

[19] Abraham Heschel, *Man Is Not Alone* (New York, NY: Harper, 1966), p. 127.

[20] T.S. Eliot, *Four Quartets* (New York, NY: Houghton Mifflin, 1943), p. 20.

[21] Patrick Kavanagh, *Collected Poems* (New York, NY: W.W. Norton & Company, 1964), p. 160.

[22] This phrase is quoted in William Cavanaugh's important short work called *Being Consumed: Economics and Christian Desire* (Grand Rapids: Eerdmans, 2008). These insights are also elaborated upon in my book *Wholeheartedness: Busyness, Exhaustion, and Healing the Divided Self* (Grand Rapids, MI: Eerdmans, 2016), pp. 16-20.

[23] Cornelius Plantinga, *Not The Ways It's Supposed to Be: A Breviary On Sin* (Grand Rapids, MI: Eerdmans, 1995), pp. 34-35.

[24] See DeGroat, *Wholeheartedness.*

[25] Shakespeare, *King Lear,* Act 5, Scene 3, p. 17 at http://nfs.sparknotes.com/lear/page_310.html

[26] John Calvin, *Institutes of the Christian Religion,* 3.2.1

[27] Thomas Merton. *Choosing to Love the World: On Contemplation.* Sydney: Read How You Want, 2008.

[28] James Finley. *Merton's Palace of Nowhere* (Notre Dame, IN: Ave Maria Press, 1978).

[29] John Stott. *The Cross of Christ* (Downers Grove, IL: Intervarsity Press, 2005).

[30] David Tracy, *The Analogical Imagination* (New York, NY: Crossroad, 1981), p. 78.

Made in the USA
Monee, IL
30 January 2020

21076005R00066